BAREFOOT BOOKS

WORLD ATLAS
STICKER BOOK

written by Nick Crane

illustrated by David Dean

Barefoot Books
Step inside a story

Welcome to the world!

Can you **label** all of the oceans and continents on our planet? To see even more place names, look at the pull-out map at the back of the book.

Cruise ships carry people on their travels across the oceans.

cruise ship

Big **trucks** carry items across land. It's often hard for truck drivers to get enough sleep because they work such long hours on the road.

truck

After the steam engine was invented, **paddle steamers** became a popular way to travel along rivers and across lakes.

paddle steamer

NORTH AMERICA

PACIFIC OCEAN

ATLANTIC OCEAN

Sometimes **oil tankers** crash, spilling oil into the ocean. Protecting our wildlife from this is very important.

oil tanker

Doctors and tourists use **seaplanes** because they can land on water next to remote islands without needing runways.

seaplane

SOUTH AMERICA

Freighter is another name for a container ship. This way of transporting items around the world uses the least energy.

freighter

container ship

Some **container ships** carry over 14,000 huge rectangular boxes of items.

Submarines can travel underwater and then surface when they reach their destination.

submarine

Where have you been in the world? Put a **footprint** sticker over any continent or ocean you have visited. Don't forget the continent where you live!

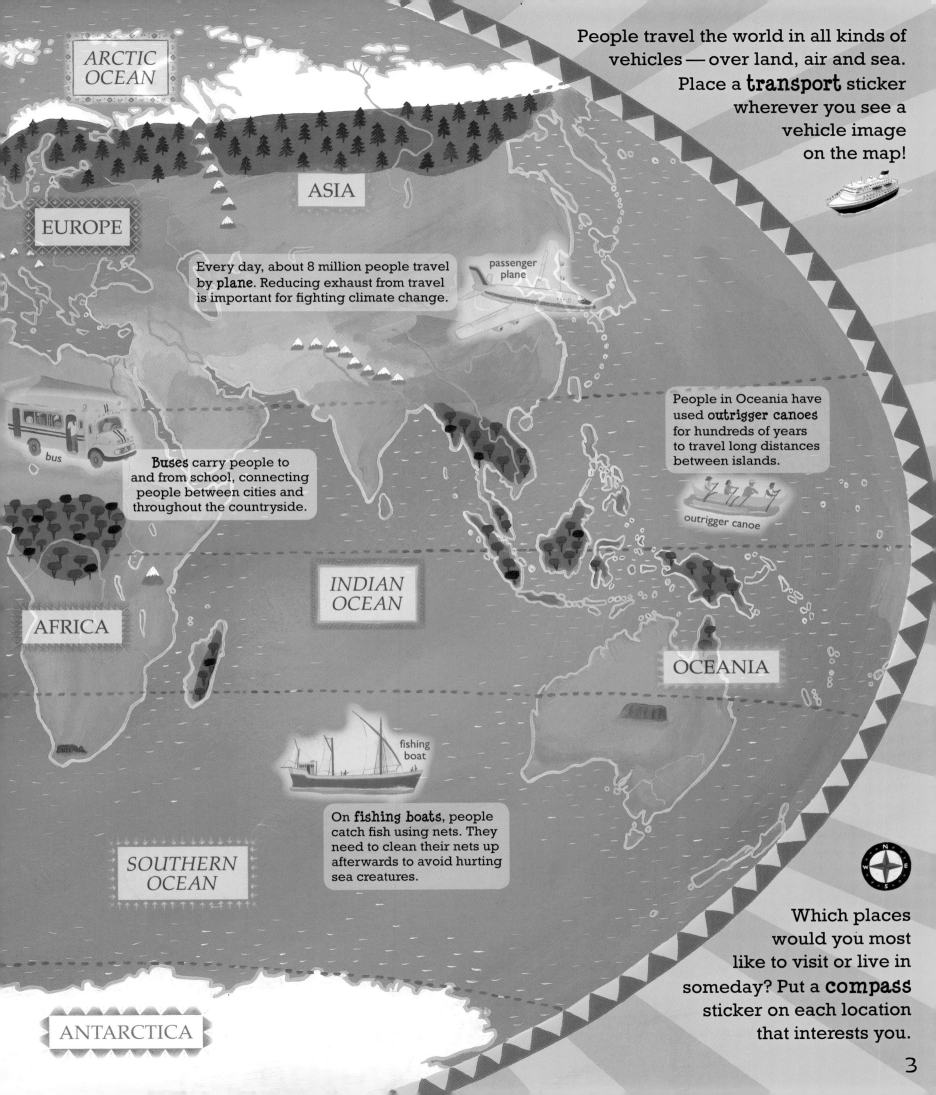

ARCTIC OCEAN

ASIA

EUROPE

Every day, about 8 million people travel by **plane**. Reducing exhaust from travel is important for fighting climate change.

passenger plane

bus

Buses carry people to and from school, connecting people between cities and throughout the countryside.

People in Oceania have used **outrigger canoes** for hundreds of years to travel long distances between islands.

outrigger canoe

AFRICA

INDIAN OCEAN

OCEANIA

fishing boat

On **fishing boats**, people catch fish using nets. They need to clean their nets up afterwards to avoid hurting sea creatures.

SOUTHERN OCEAN

Which places would you most like to visit or live in someday? Put a **compass** sticker on each location that interests you.

ANTARCTICA

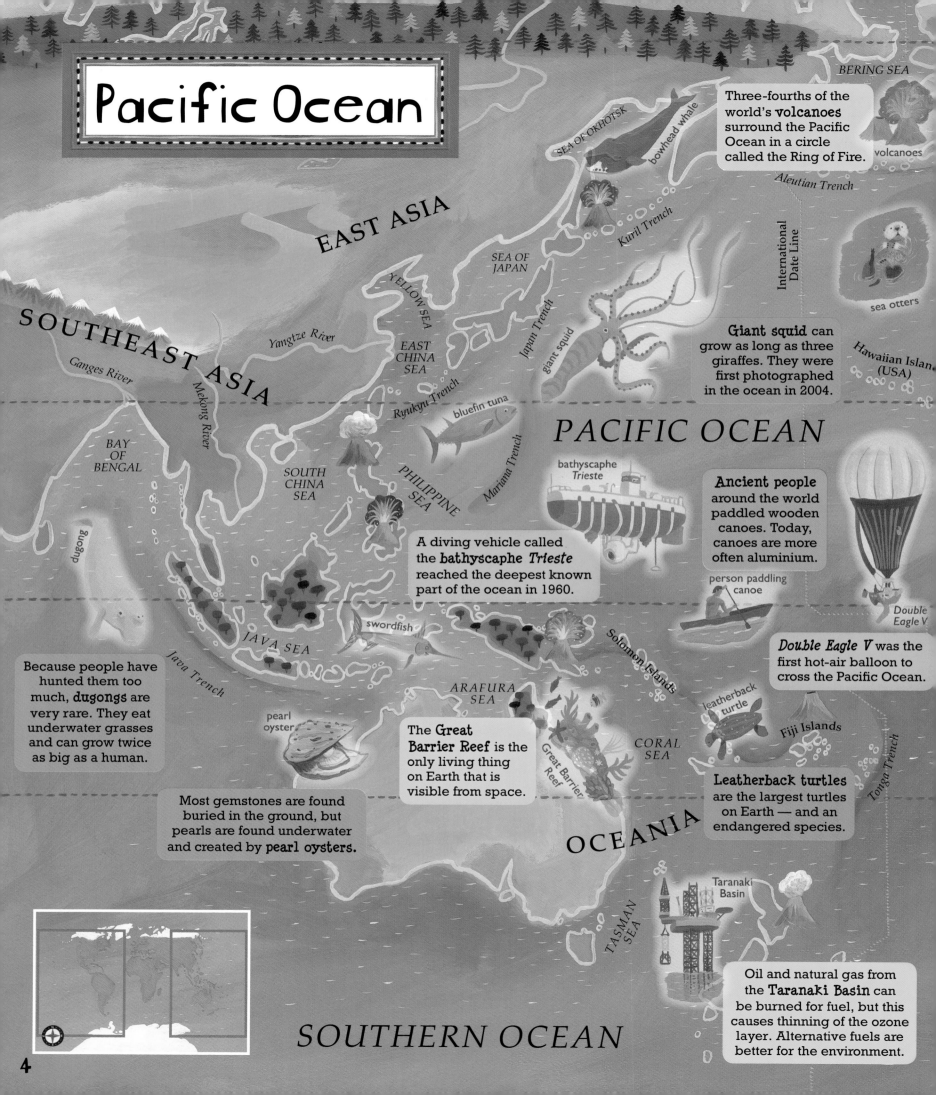

Pacific Ocean

BERING SEA

SEA OF OKHOTSK

bowhead whale

Three-fourths of the world's **volcanoes** surround the Pacific Ocean in a circle called the Ring of Fire.

volcanoes

Aleutian Trench

EAST ASIA

Kuril Trench

SEA OF JAPAN

International Date Line

sea otters

YELLOW SEA

Yangtze River

EAST CHINA SEA

Japan Trench

giant squid

Giant squid can grow as long as three giraffes. They were first photographed in the ocean in 2004.

Hawaiian Islands (USA)

SOUTHEAST ASIA

Ganges River

Mekong River

Ryukyu Trench

bluefin tuna

PACIFIC OCEAN

BAY OF BENGAL

SOUTH CHINA SEA

PHILIPPINE SEA

Mariana Trench

bathyscaphe *Trieste*

Ancient people around the world paddled wooden canoes. Today, canoes are more often aluminium.

dugong

A diving vehicle called the bathyscaphe *Trieste* reached the deepest known part of the ocean in 1960.

person paddling canoe

Double Eagle V

Because people have hunted them too much, **dugongs** are very rare. They eat underwater grasses and can grow twice as big as a human.

Java Trench

JAVA SEA

swordfish

Solomon Islands

Double Eagle V was the first hot-air balloon to cross the Pacific Ocean.

pearl oyster

ARAFURA SEA

leatherback turtle

Fiji Islands

Tonga Trench

The **Great Barrier Reef** is the only living thing on Earth that is visible from space.

Great Barrier Reef

CORAL SEA

Leatherback turtles are the largest turtles on Earth — and an endangered species.

Most gemstones are found buried in the ground, but pearls are found underwater and created by **pearl oysters.**

OCEANIA

TASMAN SEA

Taranaki Basin

Oil and natural gas from the **Taranaki Basin** can be burned for fuel, but this causes thinning of the ozone layer. Alternative fuels are better for the environment.

SOUTHERN OCEAN

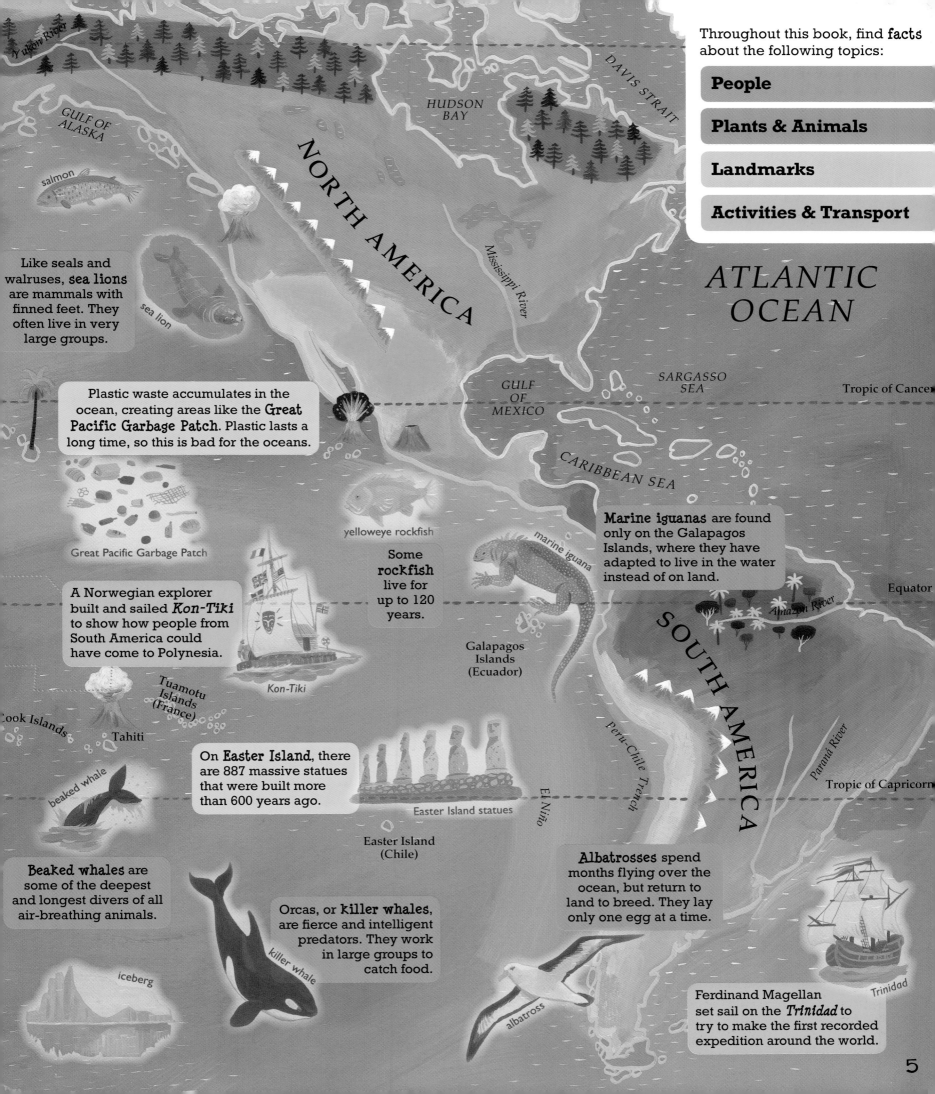

Throughout this book, find **facts** about the following topics:

People

Plants & Animals

Landmarks

Activities & Transport

Yukon River

GULF OF ALASKA

HUDSON BAY

DAVIS STRAIT

NORTH AMERICA

Mississippi River

ATLANTIC OCEAN

SARGASSO SEA

GULF OF MEXICO

Tropic of Cancer

CARIBBEAN SEA

salmon

sea lion

Like seals and walruses, **sea lions** are mammals with finned feet. They often live in very large groups.

Plastic waste accumulates in the ocean, creating areas like the **Great Pacific Garbage Patch**. Plastic lasts a long time, so this is bad for the oceans.

Great Pacific Garbage Patch

yelloweye rockfish

Some **rockfish** live for up to 120 years.

marine iguana

Marine iguanas are found only on the Galapagos Islands, where they have adapted to live in the water instead of on land.

Equator

Amazon River

SOUTH AMERICA

A Norwegian explorer built and sailed *Kon-Tiki* to show how people from South America could have come to Polynesia.

Kon-Tiki

Galapagos Islands (Ecuador)

Tuamotu Islands (France)

Cook Islands

Tahiti

On **Easter Island**, there are 887 massive statues that were built more than 600 years ago.

Easter Island statues

El Niño

Peru-Chile Trench

Paraná River

Tropic of Capricorn

beaked whale

Easter Island (Chile)

Beaked whales are some of the deepest and longest divers of all air-breathing animals.

Albatrosses spend months flying over the ocean, but return to land to breed. They lay only one egg at a time.

Orcas, or **killer whales**, are fierce and intelligent predators. They work in large groups to catch food.

iceberg

killer whale

albatross

Trinidad

Ferdinand Magellan set sail on the *Trinidad* to try to make the first recorded expedition around the world.

5

PACIFIC OCEAN

Winter Ice

BERING SEA

SEA OF OKHOTSK

GULF OF ALASKA

peregrine falcon

The **Nenets people** live in the Siberian Arctic. Many Nenets people herd reindeer for a living.

NORTH ASIA

Trans-Alaska pipeline

The **Trans-Alaska pipeline** is one of the world's biggest oil pipeline systems.

Yukon River

BERING STRAIT

CHUKCHI SEA

Yup'ik mask

The **Yup'ik people** of Alaska and Siberia are known for their art of mask making.

Summer Ice

EAST SIBERIAN SEA

Nenets people

Lena River

Mackenzie River

NORTH AMERICA

BEAUFORT SEA

polar bear

Scientists can study the Arctic Ocean on **drift stations**, set up on sheets of floating ice.

Arctic drift station

Icebreakers are huge boats that drive onto ice so that it breaks and can be pushed aside.

Summer Ice

LAPTEV SEA

Grey wolves live in packs who are like close families.

grey wolf

ARCTIC OCEAN

icebreaker

Gjøa

musk ox

The **Arctic fox**'s fur is white in the winter and turns brown in the summer.

North Pole

Severnaya Zemlya (Russia)

Yenisey River

An explorer tried to reach the North Pole by letting his ship, **Fram**, freeze and then drift in ice.

Fram

snow goose

Baffin Island (Canada)

BAFFIN BAY

Arctic fox

Novaya Zemlya (Russia)

KARA SEA

walrus

Because humans hunt them for their tusks and blubber, **walruses** have become endangered.

GREENLAND

narwhal

The **Inuit** are a group of peoples who live in the Arctic regions of Canada, Greenland, Siberia and Alaska.

Inuit girl

Svalbard (Norway)

BARENTS SEA

Summer Ice

Winter Ice

The *aurora borealis* is also called the Northern Lights because it looks like glowing lights in the sky.

Nuuk

Arctic Circle

Uummannaq

GREENLAND SEA

Winter Ice

Winter Ice

tundra swan

Ob River

aurora borealis

Beluga whales are known for their unique white skin.

beluga whale

ATLANTIC OCEAN

ICELAND

NORWEGIAN SEA

Arctic Ocean

Atlantic Ocean

ARCTIC OCEAN

More than 1,000 years ago, the **Vikings** sailed across the Atlantic to settle in Greenland.

Puffins build warm and comfortable burrows for their babies, who are called pufflings.

NORTH AMERICA

puffin

Vikings

NORTH SEA

BALTIC SEA

EUROPE

Danube River

BLACK SEA

Mississippi River

haddock

In 1912, the **Titanic** sank in the Atlantic after hitting an iceberg on its first voyage.

MEDITERRANEAN SEA

Tropic of Cancer

Ann Davison spent 254 days alone when she sailed across the Atlantic on *Felicity Ann*.

GULF OF MEXICO

Atlantic cod

Felicity Ann

Mid-Atlantic Ridge

school of common dolphins

Common dolphins are very sociable animals who live in large groups called schools or pods.

Nile River

NORTH AFRICA

Humans hunt **cod** so much that cod populations are getting smaller and smaller.

CARIBBEAN SEA

Niger River

ATLANTIC OCEAN

pirogue

Pirogues are small boats that people use to travel through marshes and along the shore.

Equator

Amazon River

Congo River

Equator

São Francisco River

Bottlenose dolphins surface frequently to breathe through the blowholes on top of their heads.

Mid-Atlantic Ridge

SOUTHERN AFRICA

swallow

SOUTH AMERICA

Every autumn, **swallows** migrate from the UK to southern Africa for the warmth.

Zambezi River

Magellanic penguins live on the southern tip of South America and hunt fish in large groups.

bottlenose dolphin

Tropic of Capricorn

SOUTHERN OCEAN

Magellanic penguin

blue whale

Every year, **Arctic terns** fly all the way from the Arctic to Antarctica and back. This is the longest known migration of any bird.

Arctic tern

The **blue whale** is the largest animal on Earth. It is even heavier than the largest dinosaur was.

Antarctic Circle

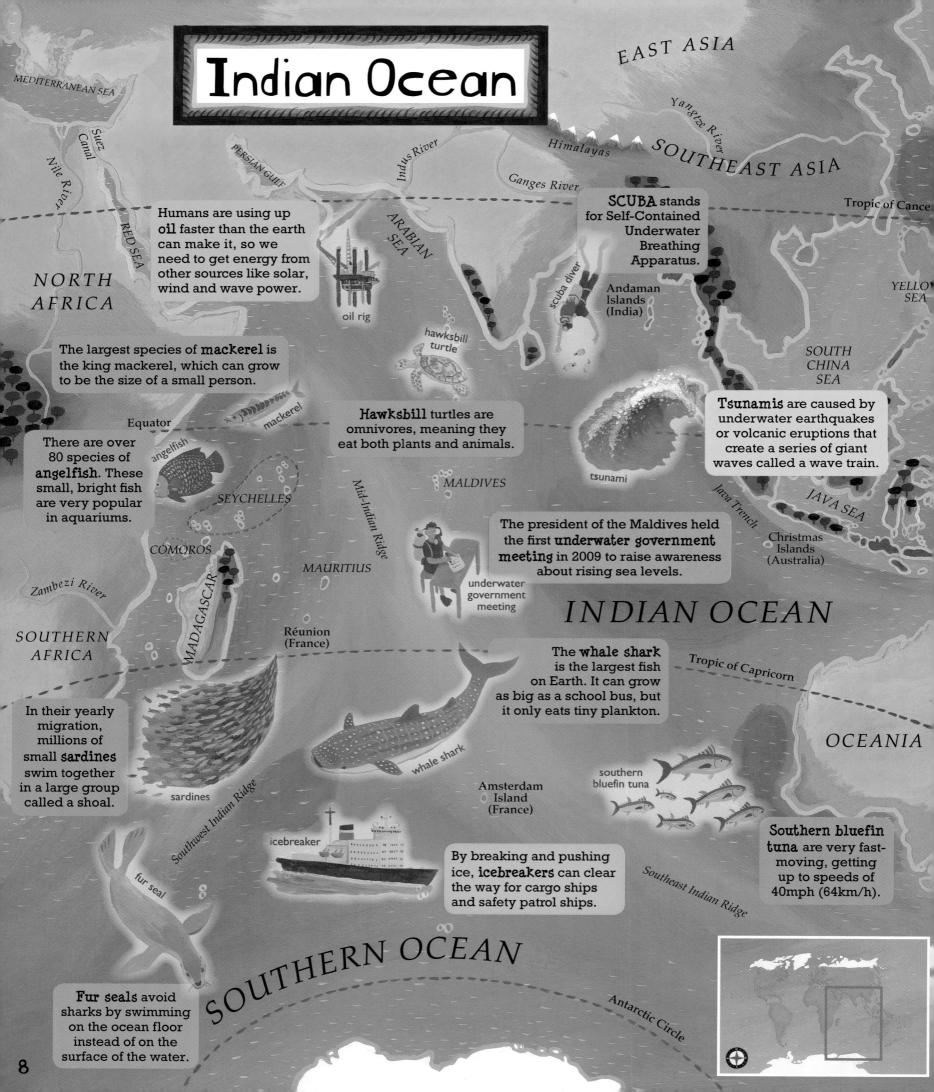

Indian Ocean

EAST ASIA

SOUTHEAST ASIA

MEDITERRANEAN SEA

Suez Canal

Nile River

RED SEA

PERSIAN GULF

Indus River

Ganges River

Himalayas

Yangtze River

Tropic of Cancer

NORTH AFRICA

ARABIAN SEA

Humans are using up **oil** faster than the earth can make it, so we need to get energy from other sources like solar, wind and wave power.

oil rig

SCUBA stands for Self-Contained Underwater Breathing Apparatus.

scuba diver

Andaman Islands (India)

YELLOW SEA

SOUTH CHINA SEA

The largest species of **mackerel** is the king mackerel, which can grow to be the size of a small person.

hawksbill turtle

Equator

mackerel

angelfish

There are over 80 species of **angelfish**. These small, bright fish are very popular in aquariums.

SEYCHELLES

Hawksbill turtles are omnivores, meaning they eat both plants and animals.

MALDIVES

tsunami

Tsunamis are caused by underwater earthquakes or volcanic eruptions that create a series of giant waves called a wave train.

Java Trench

JAVA SEA

Christmas Islands (Australia)

COMOROS

MADAGASCAR

Mid-Indian Ridge

MAURITIUS

underwater government meeting

The president of the Maldives held the first **underwater government meeting** in 2009 to raise awareness about rising sea levels.

INDIAN OCEAN

Zambezi River

SOUTHERN AFRICA

Réunion (France)

The **whale shark** is the largest fish on Earth. It can grow as big as a school bus, but it only eats tiny plankton.

Tropic of Capricorn

OCEANIA

In their yearly migration, millions of small **sardines** swim together in a large group called a shoal.

sardines

Southwest Indian Ridge

whale shark

Amsterdam Island (France)

southern bluefin tuna

icebreaker

fur seal

By breaking and pushing ice, **icebreakers** can clear the way for cargo ships and safety patrol ships.

Southeast Indian Ridge

Southern bluefin tuna are very fast-moving, getting up to speeds of 40mph (64km/h).

SOUTHERN OCEAN

Antarctic Circle

Fur seals avoid sharks by swimming on the ocean floor instead of on the surface of the water.

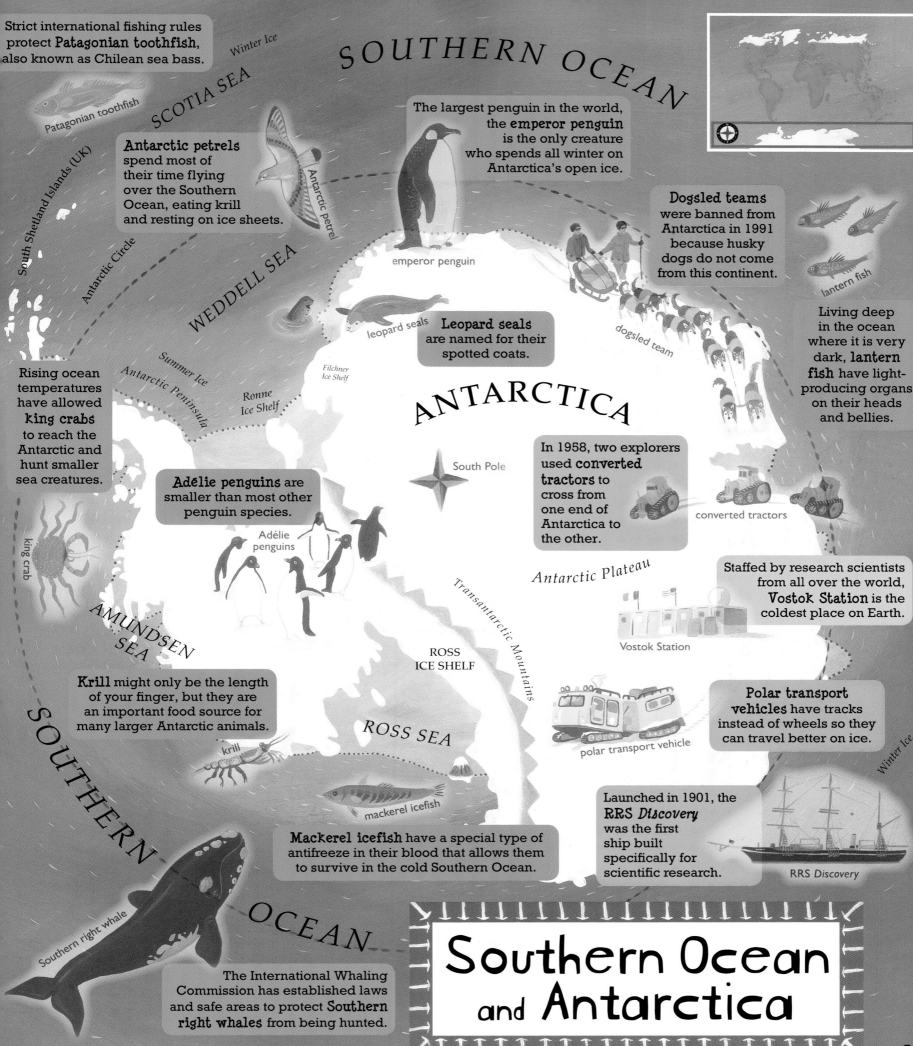

Strict international fishing rules protect **Patagonian toothfish**, also known as Chilean sea bass.

Patagonian toothfish

Winter Ice

SCOTIA SEA

SOUTHERN OCEAN

Antarctic petrels spend most of their time flying over the Southern Ocean, eating krill and resting on ice sheets.

Antarctic petrel

The largest penguin in the world, the **emperor penguin** is the only creature who spends all winter on Antarctica's open ice.

Dogsled teams were banned from Antarctica in 1991 because husky dogs do not come from this continent.

lantern fish

South Shetland Islands (UK)

Antarctic Circle

WEDDELL SEA

emperor penguin

leopard seals

Leopard seals are named for their spotted coats.

dogsled team

Living deep in the ocean where it is very dark, **lantern fish** have light-producing organs on their heads and bellies.

Rising ocean temperatures have allowed **king crabs** to reach the Antarctic and hunt smaller sea creatures.

Summer Ice

Antarctic Peninsula

Ronne Ice Shelf

Filchner Ice Shelf

ANTARCTICA

South Pole

In 1958, two explorers used **converted tractors** to cross from one end of Antarctica to the other.

converted tractors

Adélie penguins are smaller than most other penguin species.

Adélie penguins

Antarctic Plateau

Staffed by research scientists from all over the world, **Vostok Station** is the coldest place on Earth.

Vostok Station

king crab

AMUNDSEN SEA

ROSS ICE SHELF

Transantarctic Mountains

Krill might only be the length of your finger, but they are an important food source for many larger Antarctic animals.

krill

ROSS SEA

mackerel icefish

Polar transport vehicles have tracks instead of wheels so they can travel better on ice.

polar transport vehicle

Winter Ice

Launched in 1901, the RRS *Discovery* was the first ship built specifically for scientific research.

RRS Discovery

Mackerel icefish have a special type of antifreeze in their blood that allows them to survive in the cold Southern Ocean.

SOUTHERN OCEAN

Southern right whale

The International Whaling Commission has established laws and safe areas to protect **Southern right whales** from being hunted.

Southern Ocean and Antarctica

People

Teams of these **athletes** from New Zealand, Fiji, Samoa and Tonga perform ritual dances before their games.

Who flies to provide medical care to people in remote and rural regions?

Plants & Animals

Which **predator** attacks by jumping out of the water to catch its prey?

Babies of this **animal** are called joeys and they live inside their mothers' pouches.

Which **mammal** swims by paddling its webbed front feet and steering with its rear feet and tail?

Landmarks

Where can you find Central Park, a tall skyscraper with a triangular top?

Can you find this **sandstone rock formation** that is sacred to Indigenous Australians?

Activities & Transport

In Vanuatu, this carved **instrument** is an important part of many ceremonies.

EAST ASIA

Bonin Islands (Japan)

Volcano Islands (Japan)

Oceania

Mariana Islands (USA)

Hagåtña

Guam (USA)

PHILIPPINE SEA

SOUTH CHINA SEA

FEDERATED STATES OF MICRONESIA

Palikir

Many larger species of **tuna** are endangered because of overfishing.

tuna

The **king bird of paradise** is the smallest of the birds of paradise. It is about the same length as a large banana.

king bird of paradise

SOUTHEAST ASIA

PAPUA NEW GUINEA

Port Moresby

Honia

Sheep are raised throughout Australia and New Zealand for their warm wool and their meat.

Daintree Rainforest

sheep farmer

Mount Kosciuszko, Australia's highest peak, is part of the **Great Dividing Range.**

CORA SEA

flying doctors

kangaroo

Great Dividing Range

Uluru (Ayers Rock)

gold mining

opal mining

Darling River

Canberra

AUSTRALIA

Murray River

Sydney Opera House

Perth skyline

GREAT AUSTRALIAN BIGHT

wine making

platypus

The **Sydney Opera House** was designed to look like the sails of a ship floating over the water.

Australia's many types of climate and soil can produce all the major kinds of **wine.**

great white shark

Tasmania (Australia)

TASMAN SEA

SOUTHERN OCEAN

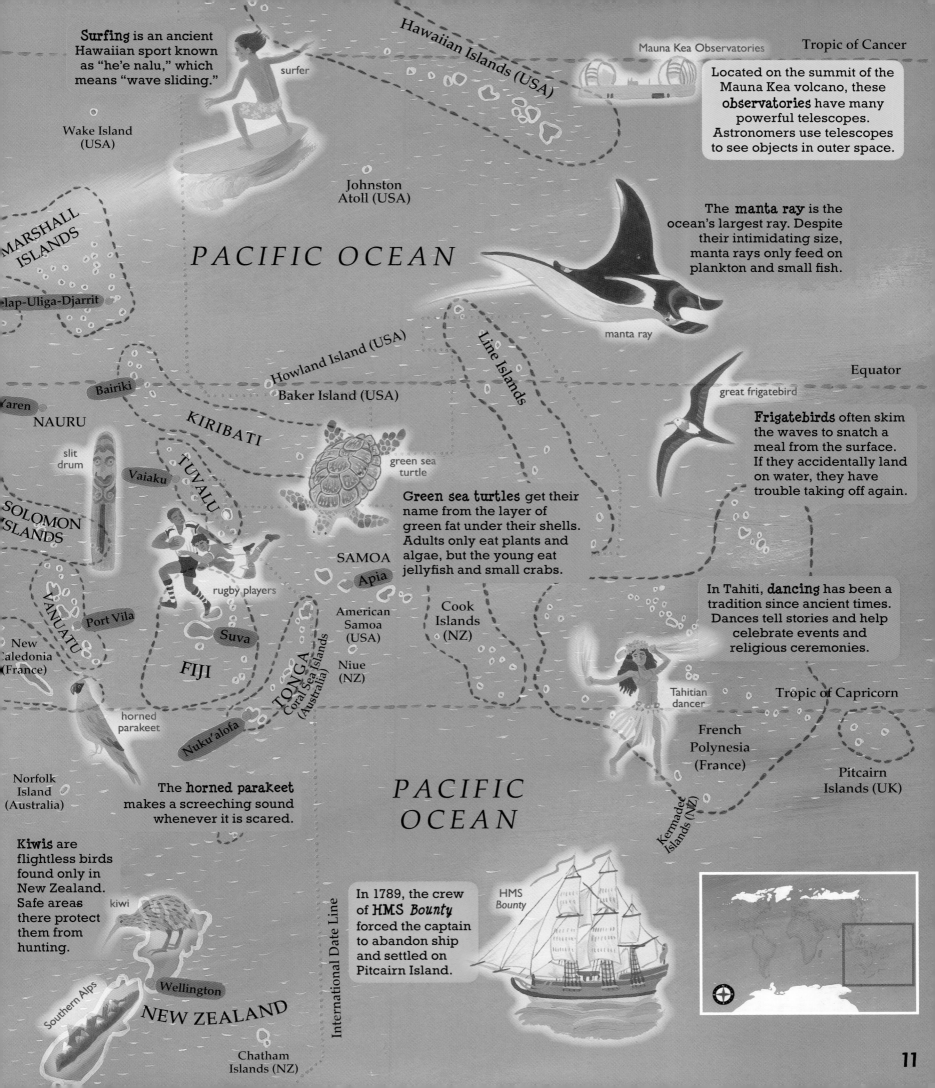

Surfing is an ancient Hawaiian sport known as "he'e nalu," which means "wave sliding."

surfer

Hawaiian Islands (USA)

Mauna Kea Observatories

Tropic of Cancer

Located on the summit of the Mauna Kea volcano, these **observatories** have many powerful telescopes. Astronomers use telescopes to see objects in outer space.

Wake Island (USA)

Johnston Atoll (USA)

PACIFIC OCEAN

MARSHALL ISLANDS

-lap-Uliga-Djarrit

The **manta ray** is the ocean's largest ray. Despite their intimidating size, manta rays only feed on plankton and small fish.

manta ray

Howland Island (USA)

Line Islands

Equator

Baker Island (USA)

great frigatebird

Bairiki

Yaren

NAURU

KIRIBATI

Frigatebirds often skim the waves to snatch a meal from the surface. If they accidentally land on water, they have trouble taking off again.

slit drum

Vaiaku

TUVALU

green sea turtle

SOLOMON ISLANDS

rugby players

Green sea turtles get their name from the layer of green fat under their shells. Adults only eat plants and algae, but the young eat jellyfish and small crabs.

SAMOA

Apia

VANUATU

Port Vila

Suva

FIJI

American Samoa (USA)

Cook Islands (NZ)

In Tahiti, **dancing** has been a tradition since ancient times. Dances tell stories and help celebrate events and religious ceremonies.

New Caledonia (France)

TONGA

Coral Sea Islands (Australia)

Niue (NZ)

Tahitian dancer

Tropic of Capricorn

horned parakeet

Nuku'alofa

French Polynesia (France)

Norfolk Island (Australia)

The **horned parakeet** makes a screeching sound whenever it is scared.

PACIFIC OCEAN

Pitcairn Islands (UK)

Kiwis are flightless birds found only in New Zealand. Safe areas there protect them from hunting.

kiwi

International Date Line

In 1789, the crew of **HMS** *Bounty* forced the captain to abandon ship and settled on Pitcairn Island.

HMS *Bounty*

Kermadec Islands (NZ)

Southern Alps

Wellington

NEW ZEALAND

Chatham Islands (NZ)

11

People

Can you find the **person performing** the traditional art of Bali?

Who is the **meditating figure** in this sculpture?

These **monks** follow disciplines like fasting between afternoon and dawn.

Plants & Animals

There are over 20,000 different species of this **flowering plant**.

Which **bird** is native to the small island of Sulawesi?

Landmarks

This **golden spire** is also called the Temple of the Emerald Buddha.

Can you find the **leafy temple**? Plants have grown over it for more than 500 years.

What is the name of these **twin buildings** in Kuala Lumpur? Each of them has 88 floors and 765 flights of stairs.

Activities & Transport

What are the **rickshaws with motors** called that drive around Thailand?

12

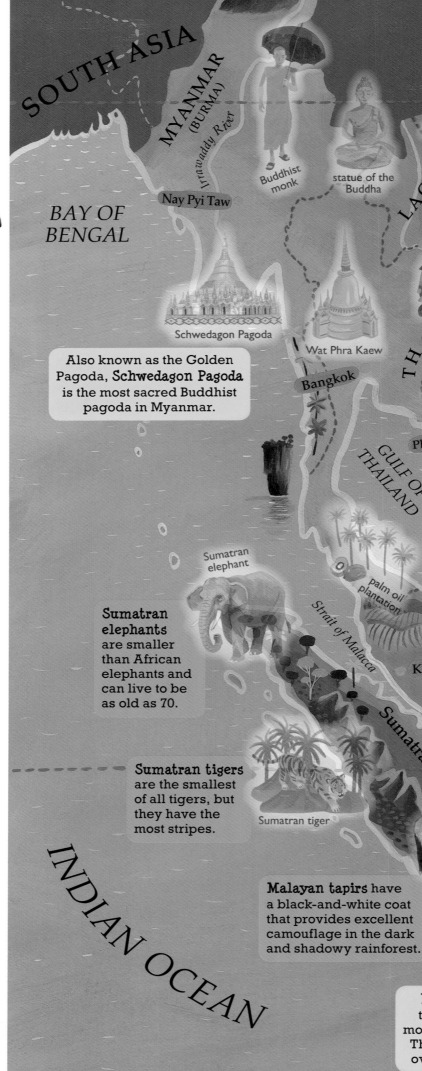

SOUTH ASIA

MYANMAR (BURMA)

Irrawaddy River

BAY OF BENGAL

Nay Pyi Taw

Buddhist monk

statue of the Buddha

Turtle Tower

Turtle Tower stands on an island in the middle of Hồ Hoàn Kiếm, which means Lake of the Returned Sword in Vietnamese.

Hà Nội

GULF OF TONKIN

LAOS

Viangchan

VIETNAM

Schwedagon Pagoda

Wat Phra Kaew

THAILAND

tŭk-tuk

Mekong River

Bangkok

Angkor Wat

Phnum Pénh

GULF OF THAILAND

CAMBODIA

Vietnamese cyclist

Also known as the Golden Pagoda, **Schwedagon Pagoda** is the most sacred Buddhist pagoda in Myanmar.

In the streets of Vietnamese cities, hundreds of thousands of **cyclists** ride next to rickshaws, cars, trucks and motorbikes.

Sumatran elephant

palm oil plantation

Petronas Towers

Sumatran elephants are smaller than African elephants and can live to be as old as 70.

Strait of Malacca

Kuala Lumpur

MALAYSIA

Sumatra

Singapore

orchid

Rajan Rive

Borneo

Sumatran tigers are the smallest of all tigers, but they have the most stripes.

Sumatran tiger

Malayan tapir

JAVA SEA

coffee plantation

INDIAN OCEAN

Malayan tapirs have a black-and-white coat that provides excellent camouflage in the dark and shadowy rainforest.

Jakarta

Jawa (Java)

Borobodur is one of the largest Buddhist monuments in the world. The complex stretches over 1.5mi² (3.88km²).

Borobodur

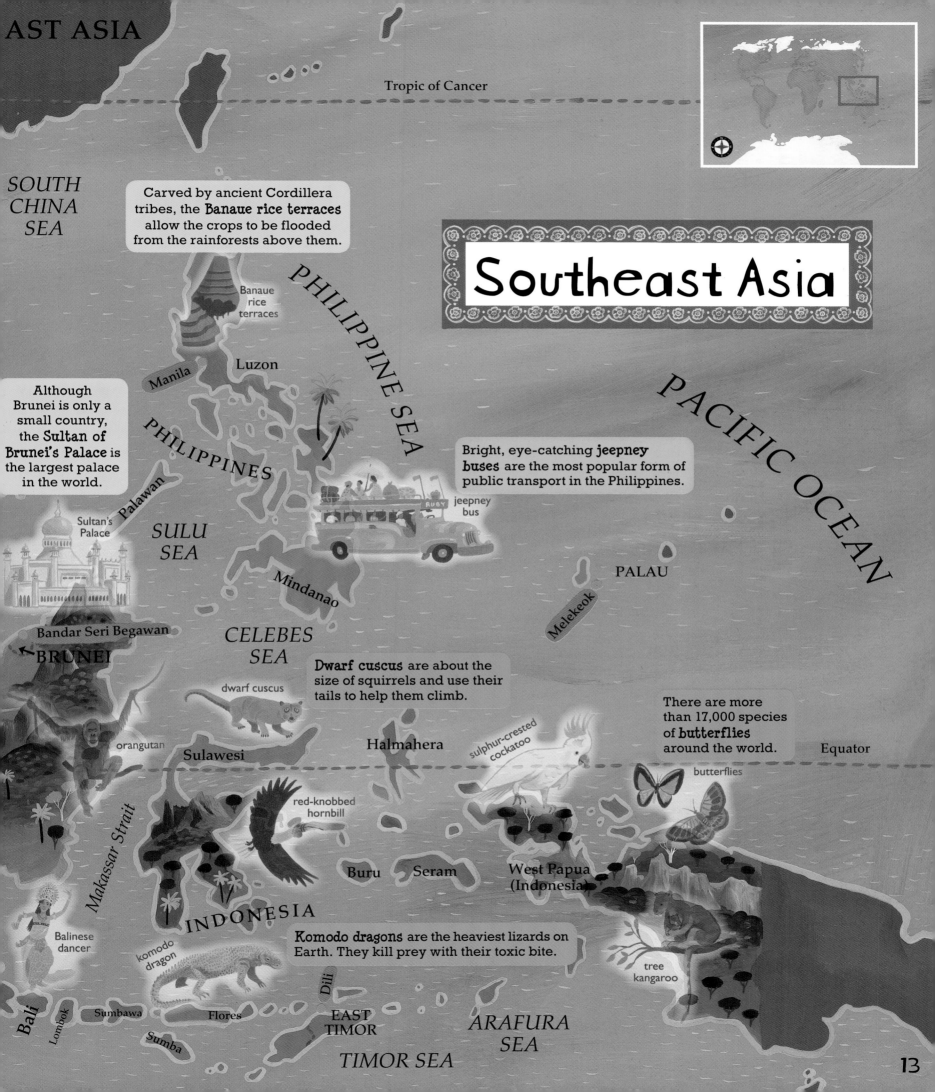

Tropic of Cancer

SOUTH
CHINA
SEA

Carved by ancient Cordillera tribes, the **Banaue rice terraces** allow the crops to be flooded from the rainforests above them.

Southeast Asia

PHILIPPINE SEA

PACIFIC OCEAN

Banaue rice terraces

Luzon

Manila

Although Brunei is only a small country, the **Sultan of Brunei's Palace** is the largest palace in the world.

PHILIPPINES

Bright, eye-catching **jeepney buses** are the most popular form of public transport in the Philippines.

jeepney bus

Palawan

Sultan's Palace

SULU SEA

Mindanao

PALAU

Melekeok

Bandar Seri Begawan

CELEBES SEA

Dwarf cuscus are about the size of squirrels and use their tails to help them climb.

BRUNEI

dwarf cuscus

There are more than 17,000 species of **butterflies** around the world.

orangutan

Sulawesi

Halmahera

sulphur-crested cockatoo

Equator

butterflies

red-knobbed hornbill

Makassar Strait

Buru   Seram   West Papua (Indonesia)

Balinese dancer

INDONESIA

Komodo dragons are the heaviest lizards on Earth. They kill prey with their toxic bite.

tree kangaroo

komodo dragon

Dili

Bali

Lombok   Sumbawa   Flores

Sumba

EAST TIMOR

ARAFURA SEA

TIMOR SEA

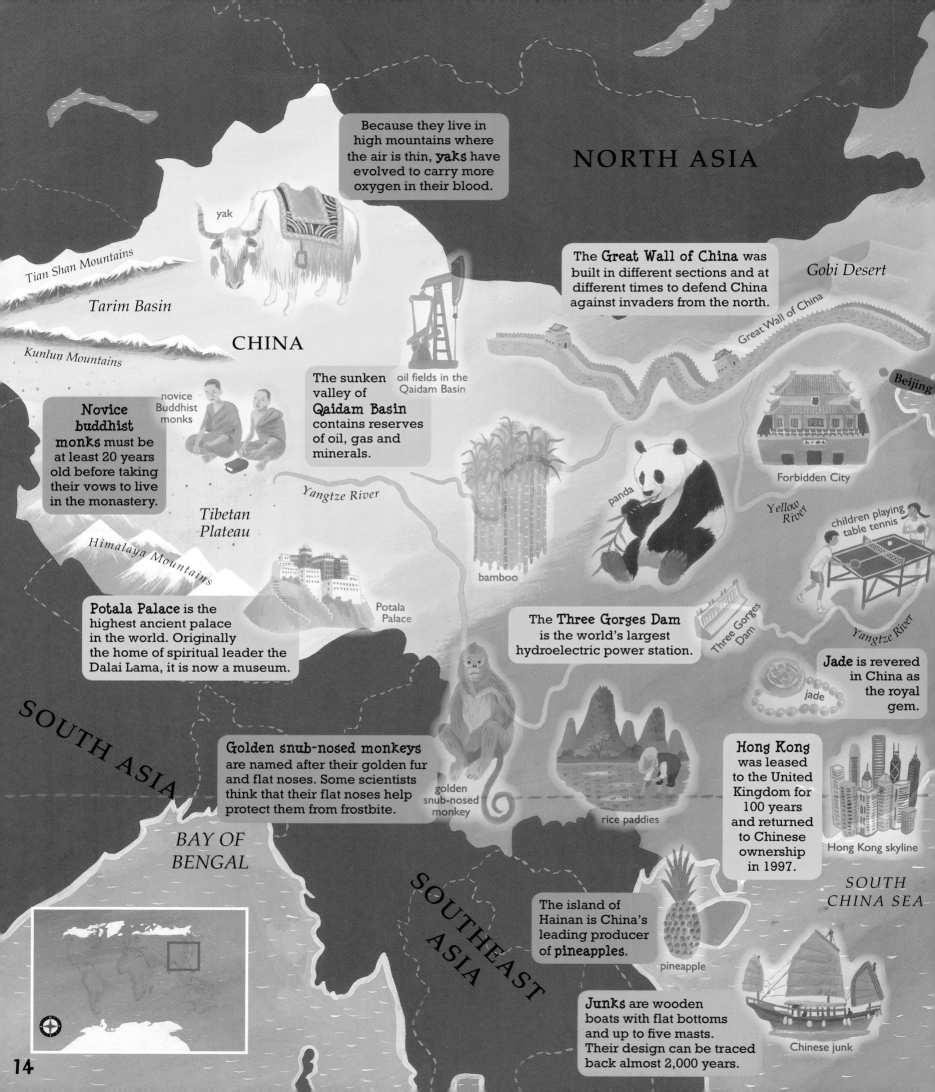

Because they live in high mountains where the air is thin, **yaks** have evolved to carry more oxygen in their blood.

NORTH ASIA

Tian Shan Mountains

Tarim Basin

yak

CHINA

Gobi Desert

The **Great Wall of China** was built in different sections and at different times to defend China against invaders from the north.

Great Wall of China

Kunlun Mountains

novice Buddhist monks

oil fields in the Qaidam Basin

The sunken valley of **Qaidam Basin** contains reserves of oil, gas and minerals.

Beijing

Novice buddhist monks must be at least 20 years old before taking their vows to live in the monastery.

Yangtze River

Tibetan Plateau

bamboo

panda

Forbidden City

Yellow River

children playing table tennis

Himalaya Mountains

Potala Palace

Potala Palace is the highest ancient palace in the world. Originally the home of spiritual leader the Dalai Lama, it is now a museum.

The **Three Gorges Dam** is the world's largest hydroelectric power station.

Three Gorges Dam

Yangtze River

Jade is revered in China as the royal gem.

jade

SOUTH ASIA

Golden snub-nosed monkeys are named after their golden fur and flat noses. Some scientists think that their flat noses help protect them from frostbite.

golden snub-nosed monkey

rice paddies

Hong Kong was leased to the United Kingdom for 100 years and returned to Chinese ownership in 1997.

Hong Kong skyline

SOUTH CHINA SEA

BAY OF BENGAL

SOUTHEAST ASIA

The island of Hainan is China's leading producer of **pineapples**.

pineapple

Junks are wooden boats with flat bottoms and up to five masts. Their design can be traced back almost 2,000 years.

Chinese junk

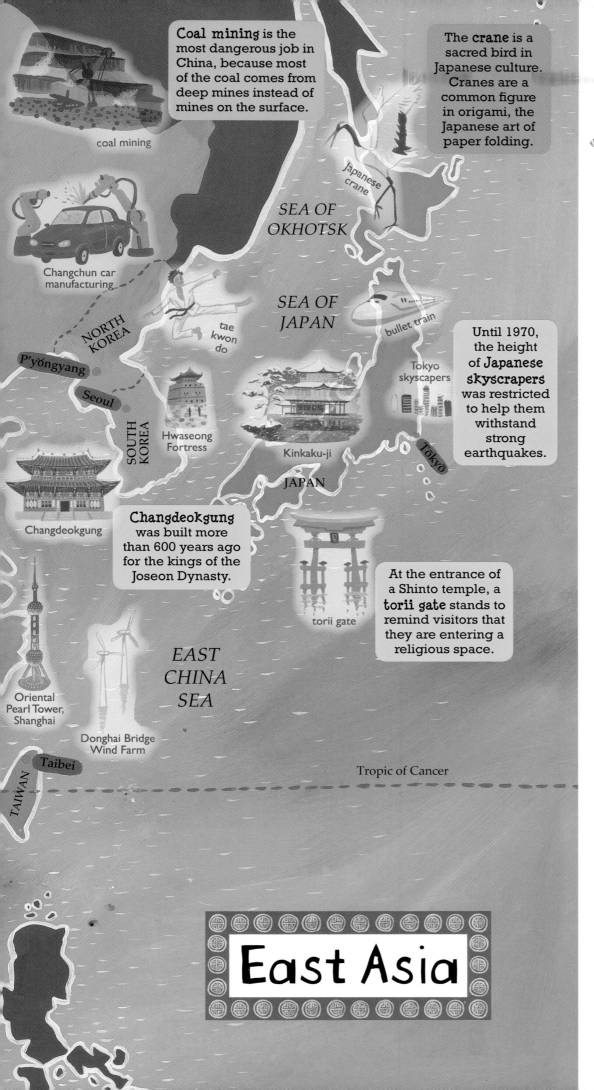

Coal **mining** is the most dangerous job in China, because most of the coal comes from deep mines instead of mines on the surface.

coal mining

The **crane** is a sacred bird in Japanese culture. Cranes are a common figure in origami, the Japanese art of paper folding.

Japanese crane

SEA OF OKHOTSK

Changchun car manufacturing

NORTH KOREA

SEA OF JAPAN

tae kwon do

bullet train

P'yŏngyang

Seoul

SOUTH KOREA

Hwaseong Fortress

Tokyo skyscrapers

Until 1970, the height of **Japanese skyscrapers** was restricted to help them withstand strong earthquakes.

Kinkaku-ji

JAPAN

Tokyo

Changdeokgung

Changdeokgung was built more than 600 years ago for the kings of the Joseon Dynasty.

At the entrance of a Shinto temple, a **torii gate** stands to remind visitors that they are entering a religious space.

torii gate

EAST CHINA SEA

Oriental Pearl Tower, Shanghai

Donghai Bridge Wind Farm

Taibei

TAIWAN

Tropic of Cancer

East Asia

People

In world tournaments for the sport these **athletes** are playing, Chinese and South Korean players win most of the medals.

Plants & Animals

These **mammals** live in cool, damp mountain regions of China. There are only a few thousand left in the wild.

Can you find the type of **giant grass** that is one of the fastest-growing plants in the world?

Landmarks

What is the name of the **palace complex** that was the private home of Chinese emperors for over 500 years?

The name of this **Zen Buddhist temple** located in Kyoto means Temple of the Golden Pavilion.

This **modern energy system** can power up to 200,000 homes.

The massive walls of this **fortress** have lookout posts, secret doors, floodgates and multiple arrow-launcher towers.

Activities & Transport

What is the English nickname for the **Shinkansen** that travels between Japan's largest cities?

The name for this **Korean martial art** roughly translates as "the art of kicking and punching."

Can you find the **flooded land** where rice grows? These fields are difficult to set up and sometimes need draining.

15

North and Central Asia

The historic **Winter Palace** is now a huge museum. To visit all the exhibits, you would have to walk over six miles (10km).

Winter Palace, Saint Petersburg

Snowy owls use their excellent eyesight, hearing and camouflage to hunt throughout the Arctic.

snowy owl

The **reindeer** is one of the only species of deer whose females have antlers.

reindeer

EUROPE

Moscow

ballerina

Saint Basil's Cathedral

European mink

Ural Mountains

The **Urengoy gas field** is the biggest source of natural gas in Russia.

Ob' River

Yenisey River

RUSSIAN FEDERATION

Urengoy gas field

Volga River

wheat

combine harvester

The **pumpjack**, used in drilling oil, has many nicknames, including "nodding donkey" and "thirsty bird."

Trans-Siberian Railway

Since 1967, the **Soyuz rocket** has launched over 1,700 spacecraft.

pumpjack

Combine harvesters cut grain and prepare it to be ground into flour.

CASPIAN SEA

KAZAKHSTAN

ARAL SEA

Soyuz rocket

Astana

Dalmatian pelican

MONGOLIA

UZBEKISTAN

Turkmen boy

petroglyphs

The **people of Turkmenistan** became independent from the Soviet Union in 1991.

TURKMENISTAN

Tashkent

Genghis Khan

Ashkhabad

Sher-Dor Madrasah

■ Samarqand

Bishkek

yurt

SOUTHWEST ASIA

Dushanbe

TAJIKISTAN

KYRGYZSTAN

Yurts are traditionally used by nomadic tribes — groups of people who often move their homes.

From 1206 to 1227, **Genghis Khan** ruled the Mongol Empire, which stretched over much of northern and central Asia.

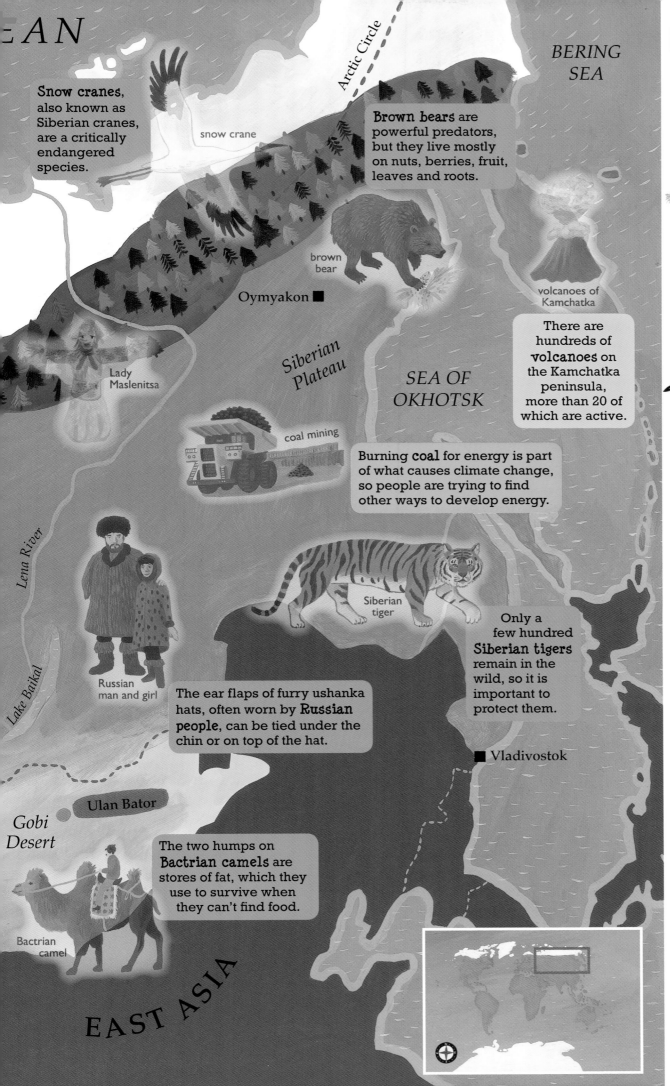

EAN

BERING SEA

Arctic Circle

Snow cranes, also known as Siberian cranes, are a critically endangered species.

snow crane

Brown bears are powerful predators, but they live mostly on nuts, berries, fruit, leaves and roots.

brown bear

Oymyakon ■

volcanoes of Kamchatka

Lady Maslenitsa

Siberian Plateau

SEA OF OKHOTSK

There are hundreds of volcanoes on the Kamchatka peninsula, more than 20 of which are active.

coal mining

Burning coal for energy is part of what causes climate change, so people are trying to find other ways to develop energy.

Lena River

Russian man and girl

Siberian tiger

Only a few hundred Siberian tigers remain in the wild, so it is important to protect them.

Lake Baikal

The ear flaps of furry ushanka hats, often worn by Russian people, can be tied under the chin or on top of the hat.

■ Vladivostok

Ulan Bator

Gobi Desert

The two humps on Bactrian camels are stores of fat, which they use to survive when they can't find food.

Bactrian camel

EAST ASIA

People

Who is performing an Italian and French dance that became an important tradition in Russia?

Before they fast for Lent, Russian Orthodox Christians eat blini (pancakes) and burn this scarecrow-like figure.

Plants & Animals

Which endangered species has a fur coat that helps keep it warm in cold water?

This rare, large bird is one of the world's heaviest animals that can still fly.

Which grain produced in Russia can be used to make many different kinds of food?

Landmarks

Some say that this unique cathedral in Moscow looks like the flames of a bonfire reaching into the sky.

Traditionally, madrasahs like this one were places where young children learned about Islam.

Activities & Transport

It takes about seven days to travel across Russia on this train line, the longest in the world.

Can you find the ancient rock carvings made by early humans?

17

People

In rural areas, this **person** might spend 6 hours a day carrying a heavy pot that she balances on her head.

This **girl** comes from a culture whose written history dates back over 3,000 years.

Plants & Animals

Which **bird** gets a ride with a buffalo in exchange for eating the insects that buzz around it?

 Siddhartha Gautama, the founder of Buddhism, achieved enlightenment under **this**, also known as the Bodhi Tree.

What is the national tree of India? It grows horizontally by sprouting roots from its branches, which then touch the ground and become like another trunk.

 These beautiful **grey cats** are becoming increasingly rare; only around 6,000 of them survive in the wild. Several conservation projects are working to protect their habitats.

Landmarks

Which **building** holds the tombs of two founders of Pakistan and the country's first prime minister?

 Many of these older **dwellings** are painted blue. Historians don't know exactly why.

Can you find the massive **dome structure** that is one of the largest places of meditation in Nepal?

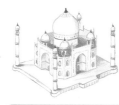 This **huge complex** took nearly twenty years to complete and required the combined skill of over 20,000 workers from across India.

Activities & Transport

The **sport** this boy is playing is the second most popular one in the world. It is played in a variety of formats, and one match can last days.

18

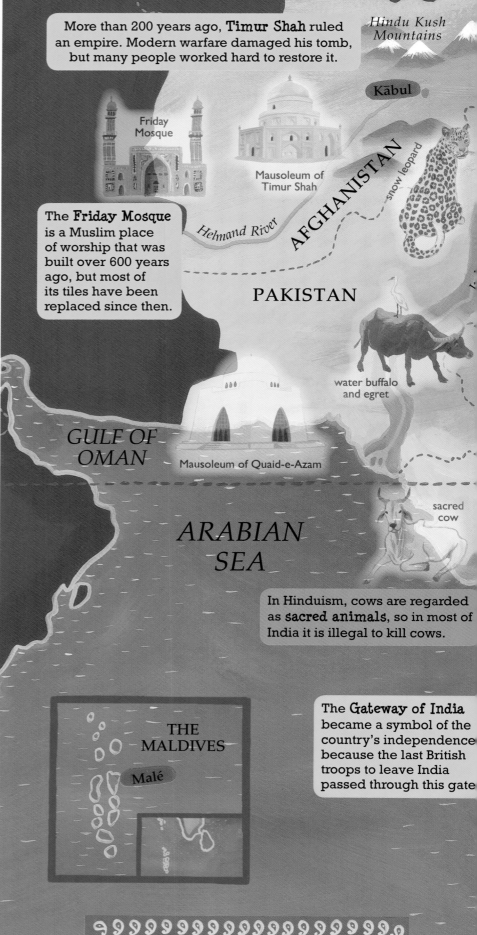

More than 200 years ago, **Timur Shah** ruled an empire. Modern warfare damaged his tomb, but many people worked hard to restore it.

Hindu Kush Mountains

Kabul

Friday Mosque

Mausoleum of Timur Shah

snow leopard

Helmand River

AFGHANISTAN

The **Friday Mosque** is a Muslim place of worship that was built over 600 years ago, but most of its tiles have been replaced since then.

PAKISTAN

water buffalo and egret

GULF OF OMAN

Mausoleum of Quaid-e-Azam

sacred cow

ARABIAN SEA

In Hinduism, cows are regarded as **sacred animals**, so in most of India it is illegal to kill cows.

THE MALDIVES

Malé

The **Gateway of India** became a symbol of the country's independence because the last British troops to leave India passed through this gate

South Asia

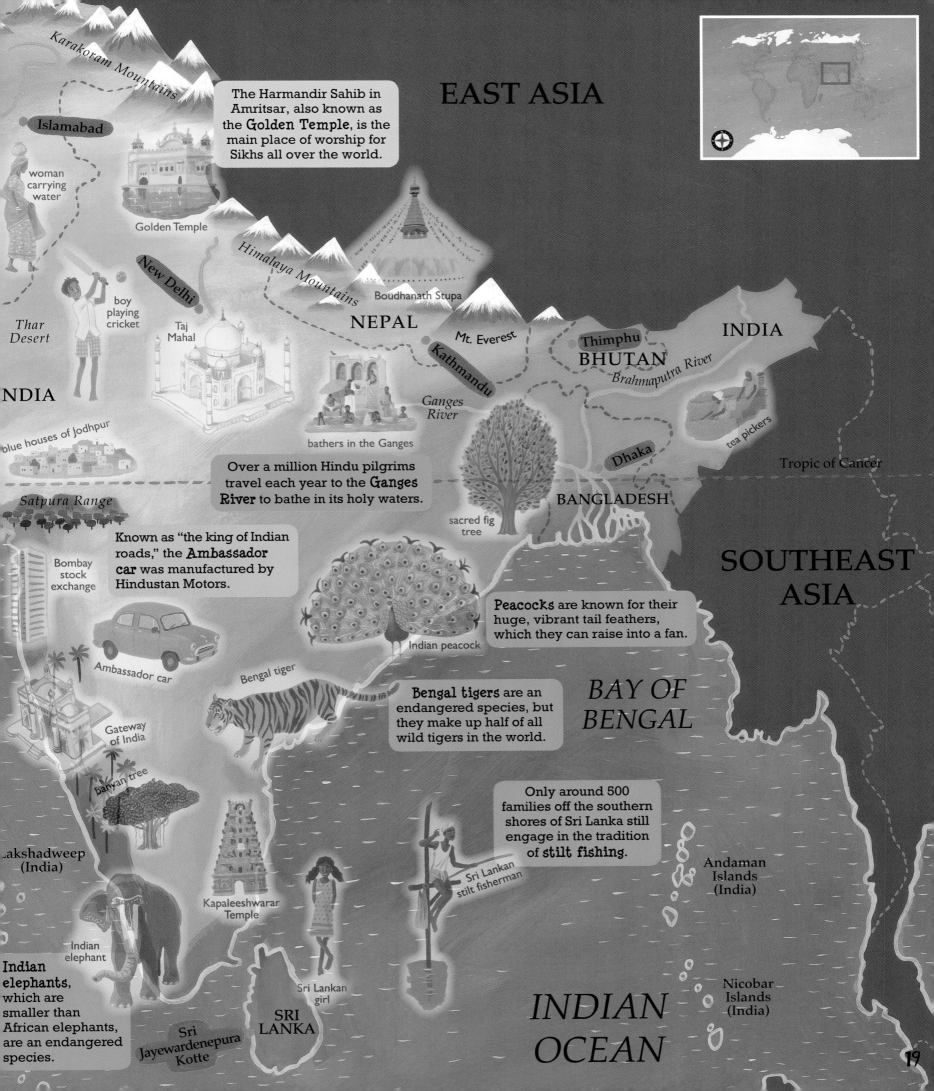

Karakoram Mountains

Islamabad

woman carrying water

Golden Temple

The Harmandir Sahib in Amritsar, also known as the **Golden Temple**, is the main place of worship for Sikhs all over the world.

Himalaya Mountains

Boudhanath Stupa

New Delhi

boy playing cricket

Taj Mahal

NEPAL

Mt. Everest

Thimphu

BHUTAN

INDIA

Thar Desert

Brahmaputra River

Kathmandu

NDIA

Ganges River

tea pickers

blue houses of Jodhpur

bathers in the Ganges

Dhaka

Tropic of Cancer

Satpura Range

Over a million Hindu pilgrims travel each year to the **Ganges River** to bathe in its holy waters.

BANGLADESH

Known as "the king of Indian roads," the **Ambassador car** was manufactured by Hindustan Motors.

sacred fig tree

SOUTHEAST ASIA

Bombay stock exchange

Peacocks are known for their huge, vibrant tail feathers, which they can raise into a fan.

Indian peacock

Ambassador car

Bengal tiger

Bengal tigers are an endangered species, but they make up half of all wild tigers in the world.

BAY OF BENGAL

Gateway of India

banyan tree

Only around 500 families off the southern shores of Sri Lanka still engage in the tradition of **stilt fishing**.

Lakshadweep (India)

Kapaleeshwarar Temple

Sri Lankan stilt fisherman

Andaman Islands (India)

Indian elephant

Sri Lankan girl

Indian elephants, which are smaller than African elephants, are an endangered species.

Sri Jayewardenepura Kotte

SRI LANKA

Nicobar Islands (India)

INDIAN OCEAN

People

This **man** wears a traditional dagger called a khanjar for special ceremonies.

Plants & Animals

These **animals** are often compared to dogs, but they are more closely related to cats.

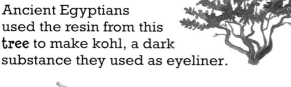

Ancient Egyptians used the resin from this **tree** to make kohl, a dark substance they used as eyeliner.

Seeds and flowers combine to make this sweet **fruit**, one of the first foods humans ever grew.

Landmarks

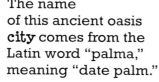

What is the name of the **luxurious hotel** that sits on an artificial island in the Persian Gulf?

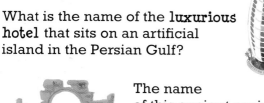

The name of this ancient oasis **city** comes from the Latin word "palma," meaning "date palm."

Can you find this giant limestone **stairway** that links two sides of the capital city of Yerevan?

This **mosque** has six minarets — high towers from which Muslims are called to prayer.

Activities & Transport

The largest in the world of **these** are in the Persian Gulf.

Because of their small size, these **boats** are often used in rescue missions.

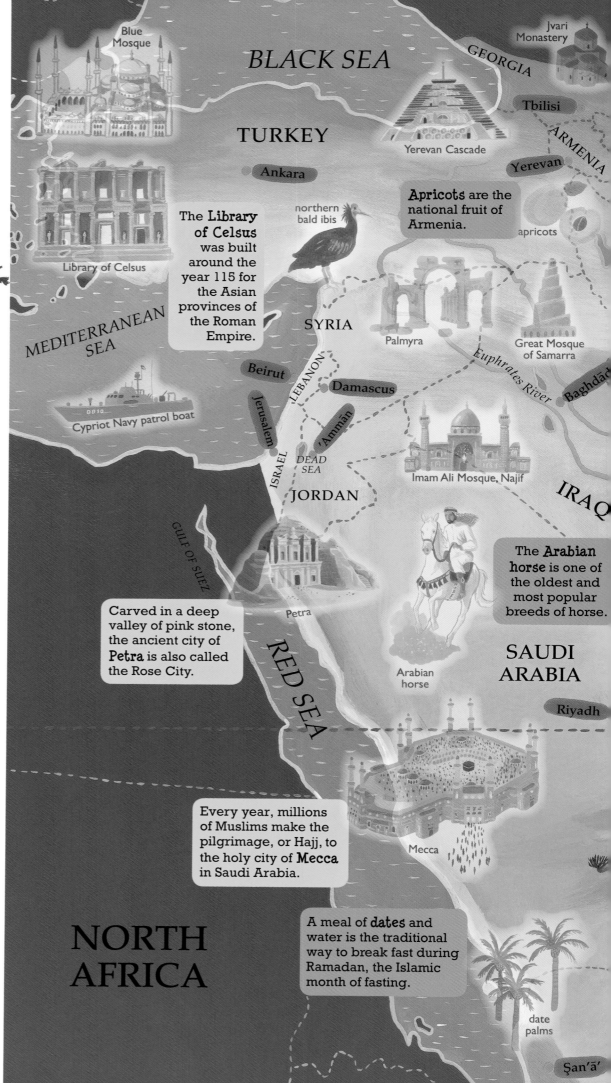

BLACK SEA

GEORGIA

Blue Mosque

Jvari Monastery

TURKEY

Yerevan Cascade

Tbilisi

ARMENIA

Ankara

Yerevan

Apricots are the national fruit of Armenia.

northern bald ibis

apricots

The **Library of Celsus** was built around the year 115 for the Asian provinces of the Roman Empire.

Library of Celsus

SYRIA

Palmyra

Great Mosque of Samarra

MEDITERRANEAN SEA

Beirut

LEBANON

Damascus

Euphrates River

Baghdād

Cypriot Navy patrol boat

Jerusalem

ISRAEL

'Amman

DEAD SEA

Imam Ali Mosque, Najif

IRAQ

JORDAN

GULF OF SUEZ

Carved in a deep valley of pink stone, the ancient city of **Petra** is also called the Rose City.

Petra

Arabian horse

The **Arabian horse** is one of the oldest and most popular breeds of horse.

SAUDI ARABIA

Riyadh

RED SEA

Every year, millions of Muslims make the pilgrimage, or Hajj, to the holy city of **Mecca** in Saudi Arabia.

Mecca

NORTH AFRICA

A meal of **dates** and water is the traditional way to break fast during Ramadan, the Islamic month of fasting.

date palms

Şan'ā'

Southwest Asia

AZERBAIJAN

CASPIAN SEA

Baki

Elborz Mountains

Tehrān

Eurasian lynx

Shah Mosque

The **Shah Mosque** is known for its four large vaulted rooms as well as its beautiful and varied mosaics.

Humans have grown **pomegranates** for more than 5,000 years.

pomegranate farm

kestrel

Known for their ability to hunt from the air, **kestrels** hover very still before swooping quickly onto their prey.

Zagros Mountains

IRAN

Tigris River

KUWAIT

Kuwait

oil fields

Burj Al Arab Hotel

Iranian girl

SOUTH ASIA

Al Manāmah

BAHRAIN

QATAR

Doha

PERSIAN GULF

Abu Dhabi

UNITED ARAB EMIRATES

GULF OF OMAN

Muscat

OMAN

During the Iranian revolution, there were restrictions on girls' education, but today 60% of **Iranian university students** are women.

Tropic of Cancer

ARABIAN SEA

fishing boat

Commercial **fishing boats** in the Arabian Sea look for the sardines, prawns and mackerel who live in coastal waters.

striped hyena

Rub' al Khali

frankincense tree

YEMEN

figs

Omani man

Old Walled City of Shibam

Sometimes called the Manhattan of the Desert, the **Old Walled City of Shibam** contains many tall buildings that are hundreds of years old. Some are even older — like one mosque that was built in 904.

People

These **performers** wear matching costumes and step in time with each other in Ukrainian tradition.

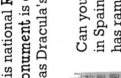

Who is the **athlete** in the Alps? This person's snow sport has existed for over 5,000 years.

Workers like this one extract coal from mines in Poland. Poland produces a lot of coal, copper, zinc and silver.

Plants & Animals

Just one month after they are born, these **animals** are capable of finding their own food, but they usually stay with their mothers until they are fully grown.

Many people use flowers from these **fields** to make things smell good or to help them sleep.

Which **fruit** is often grown in vineyards in Italy and France to be made into wine?

Landmarks

This national **Romanian** monument is often referred to as Dracula's Castle.

Can you find the **tall tower** in Spain? Instead of stairs, it has ramps wide enough for two people on horseback.

In the ancient Roman empire, many people came to watch gladiator fights, animal hunts and mock battles in this oval **arena**.

Which **building** is tilted? There are seven bells inside it, each one representing a different note on the musical scale.

What is the name of the highest and most extensive **mountain range** in Europe?

Which best-selling **toy** comes from Hungary? It was invented by an architect in the 1970s.

Activities & Transport

Half of the land in Sweden is covered by forests. Some trees are cut down to build these **structures**, but nature conservation agreements protect many others.

Each Ukrainian village and district has its own special designs for these **decorated items**.

ARCTIC OCEAN

BARENTS SEA

WHITE SEA

NORTH ASIA

Reindeer herding plays a large part in the daily life of many **Sami people**. Reindeer can provide food, clothing and labor.

Sami woman

FINLAND

Helsinki

GULF OF BOTHNIA

Europe

Arctic Circle

NORWEGIAN SEA

Oslo

NORWAY

Shetland Islands (UK)

Faroe Islands (Denmark)

Reykjavik

geyser

ICELAND

Scottish boy

The English word "**geyser**" comes from the Icelandic word "geysa," which means "to gush."

This **boy** wears rain boots because the western Highlands of Scotland get as much as 9ft (2.7m) of rain each year.

ATLANTIC OCEAN

BLACK SEA

SEA OF AZOV

SOUTHWEST ASIA

CYPRUS

Nicosia

The Parthenon was built more than 2,000 years ago to celebrate Athena, the Greek goddess of wisdom.

Crete (Greece)

MEDITERRANEAN SEA

The antlers of **fallow deer** are flat and broad, unlike the antlers of other deer.

Cossack dancer

Pysanka (decorated egg)

UKRAINE

wild boar

fallow deer

Dnieper River

Kiev

MOLDOVA

Chișinău

ROMANIA

Carpathian Mountains

Bran Castle

Bucharest

Danube River

TURKEY

BULGARIA

Sofiya

ESTONIA

LATVIA

Riga

LITHUANIA

Vilnius

Minsk

BELARUS

Saint Sophia Cathedral

Warsaw

POLAND

Skopje

MACEDONIA

GREECE

Parthenon

Athens

raspberry

Belgrade

ALBANIA

Tiranë

RUSSIAN FEDERATION

BALTIC SEA

SWEDEN

timber-frame house

miner

Rubik's Cube

SLOVAKIA

Bratislava

HUNGARY

SERBIA

Budapest

Zagreb

CROATIA

BOSNIA-HERZEGOVINA

Sarajevo

MONTENEGRO

Podgorica

Mt. Etna is a live volcano that erupts regularly, sometimes for years at a time.

Wind power is a form of energy that produces no harmful emissions or hazardous waste.

wind turbine

DENMARK

Copenhagen

Berlin

Prague

CZECH REPUBLIC

Vienna

AUSTRIA

SLOVENIA

Ljubljana

ADRIATIC SEA

skier

the Alps

Colosseum

ITALY

Mt. Etna

Sicily (Italy)

MALTA

Valletta

The **Brandenburg Gate** in Berlin was completed in 1791.

Brandenburg Gate

GERMANY

THE NETHERLANDS

Amsterdam

Brussels

BELGIUM

LUXEMBOURG

Luxembourg

FRANCE

Bern

SWITZERLAND

Leaning Tower of Pisa

VATICAN CITY

Rome

UNITED KINGDOM

Big Ben

London

ENGLISH CHANNEL

Paris

Eiffel Tower

lavender fields

Corsica (France)

Sardinia (Italy)

grapes

Sagrada Família is a basilica, or church. Its construction started in 1882 and is still unfinished.

Historians think that people built **Stonehenge** more than 4,000 years ago.

IRELAND

Dublin

Stonehenge

These **children playing football** are wearing the shirts of the Portuguese national team.

cow

Humans raise **cows** either for their milk or their meat. Cows raised for their milk are called dairy cows.

Pyrenees

SPAIN

Madrid

olive tree

olive oil

Balearic Islands (Spain)

Sagrada Família

La Giralda

children playing football

PORTUGAL

Lisbon

Olives and olive oil are popular in food in most countries near the Mediterranean Sea.

NORTH AFRICA

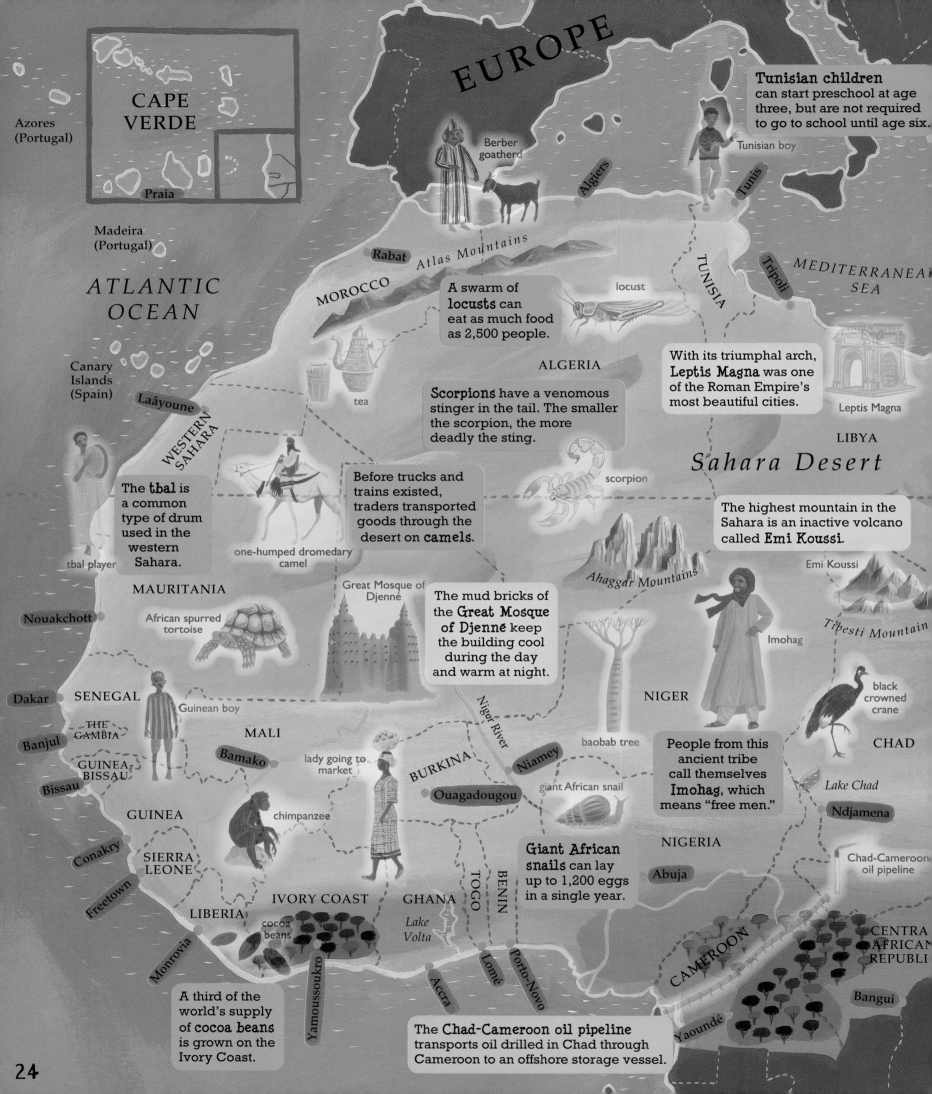

CAPE VERDE

Praia

Azores (Portugal)

Madeira (Portugal)

ATLANTIC OCEAN

Canary Islands (Spain)

EUROPE

Berber goatherd

Tunisian children can start preschool at age three, but are not required to go to school until age six.

Tunisian boy

Algiers

Rabat

Atlas Mountains

MOROCCO

A swarm of **locusts** can eat as much food as 2,500 people.

locust

ALGERIA

Scorpions have a venomous stinger in the tail. The smaller the scorpion, the more deadly the sting.

tea

TUNISIA

Tripoli

MEDITERRANEAN SEA

With its triumphal arch, **Leptis Magna** was one of the Roman Empire's most beautiful cities.

Leptis Magna

LIBYA

Sahara Desert

Laâyoune

WESTERN SAHARA

The **tbal** is a common type of drum used in the western Sahara.

tbal player

Before trucks and trains existed, traders transported goods through the desert on **camels**.

one-humped dromedary camel

scorpion

The highest mountain in the Sahara is an inactive volcano called **Emi Koussi**.

Emi Koussi

Ahaggar Mountains

Tibesti Mountain

MAURITANIA

Nouakchott

African spurred tortoise

Great Mosque of Djenné

The mud bricks of the **Great Mosque of Djenné** keep the building cool during the day and warm at night.

Imohag

NIGER

baobab tree

black crowned crane

CHAD

Dakar

SENEGAL

Guinean boy

THE GAMBIA

Banjul

GUINEA-BISSAU

Bissau

Niger River

MALI

Bamako

lady going to market

BURKINA

Niamey

Ouagadougou

giant African snail

People from this ancient tribe call themselves **Imohag**, which means "free men."

Lake Chad

Ndjamena

GUINEA

chimpanzee

Conakry

SIERRA LEONE

Freetown

LIBERIA

Monrovia

IVORY COAST

cocoa beans

Yamoussoukro

Accra

GHANA

Lake Volta

TOGO

Lomé

BENIN

Porto-Novo

NIGERIA

Abuja

Giant African snails can lay up to 1,200 eggs in a single year.

Chad-Cameroon oil pipeline

CAMEROON

Yaoundé

CENTRAL AFRICAN REPUBLIC

Bangui

A third of the world's supply of **cocoa beans** is grown on the Ivory Coast.

The **Chad-Cameroon oil pipeline** transports oil drilled in Chad through Cameroon to an offshore storage vessel.

24

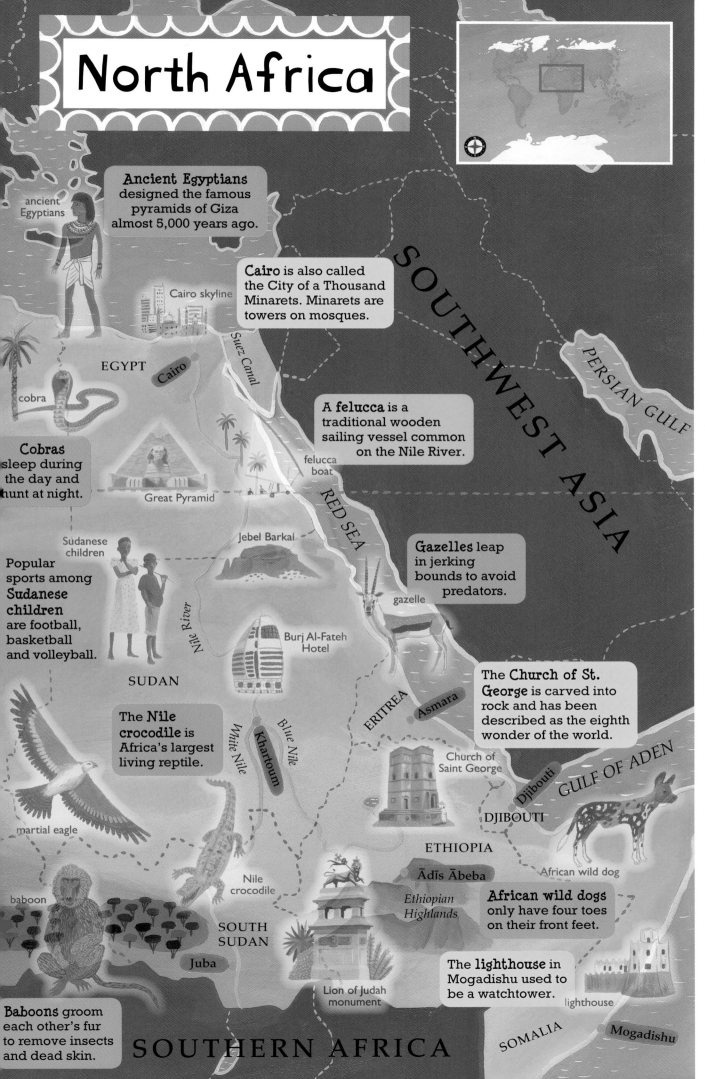

North Africa

Ancient Egyptians designed the famous pyramids of Giza almost 5,000 years ago.

ancient Egyptians

Cairo is also called the City of a Thousand Minarets. Minarets are towers on mosques.

Cairo skyline

SOUTHWEST ASIA

PERSIAN GULF

Suez Canal

EGYPT

Cairo

cobra

A **felucca** is a traditional wooden sailing vessel common on the Nile River.

felucca boat

Cobras sleep during the day and hunt at night.

Great Pyramid

RED SEA

Jebel Barkal

Sudanese children

Popular sports among **Sudanese children** are football, basketball and volleyball.

Nile River

Gazelles leap in jerking bounds to avoid predators.

gazelle

Burj Al-Fateh Hotel

The **Church of St. George** is carved into rock and has been described as the eighth wonder of the world.

SUDAN

The **Nile crocodile** is Africa's largest living reptile.

White Nile

Blue Nile

Khartoum

ERITREA

Asmara

Church of Saint George

martial eagle

Djibouti

GULF OF ADEN

DJIBOUTI

Nile crocodile

ETHIOPIA

Ādīs Ābeba

African wild dog

African wild dogs only have four toes on their front feet.

baboon

Ethiopian Highlands

SOUTH SUDAN

Juba

Lion of Judah monument

The **lighthouse** in Mogadishu used to be a watchtower.

lighthouse

Baboons groom each other's fur to remove insects and dead skin.

SOMALIA

Mogadishu

SOUTHERN AFRICA

People

Over 36 languages are spoken in this **boy**'s country.

What is the occupation of this **man** from Morocco?

This **person** is carrying food to trade with others.

Plants & Animals

Which **bird** is the largest of the African eagles?

Which **animal** has a shell over its body and digs underground?

Because this **tree** stores vast amounts of water, it is called the Tree of Life.

Landmarks

This ancient **monument** is made up of over 2 million blocks of limestone.

Which **statue** has a lion on top of it that represents the emperors of Ethiopia?

The oldest examples of hieroglyphics, the type of writing used in ancient Egypt, are on this **hill** in Sudan.

Activities & Transport

Morocco exports a lot of which **hot drink**?

People

Who travels a long way with heavy jugs? This happens when water is scarce.

These expert **hunters** are descendants of the first people ever to live on this land.

Plants & Animals

These **creatures** with trunks and tusks are the largest land animals in the world.

Can you find this **mammal**? It makes a dark red substance to protect its skin from the sun.

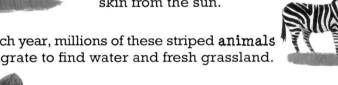

Each year, millions of these striped **animals** migrate to find water and fresh grassland.

This **fruit** from one type of palm tree provides both food and medicine.

What is the name of the freshwater **fish** who swims in Lake Malawi?

Landmarks

This **waterfall** is the largest curtain of falling water in the world.

What is the tall **mountain** in Kenya that is actually an extinct volcano?

This inactive **volcano** in Tanzania is the highest mountain on the African continent.

People can hike or take a cable car to the top of this **scenic point** and see all of Cape Town below.

Activities & Transport

This **activity** happens by hand on small farms in Kenya. Kenyan tea is famous for its excellent taste and nutrition.

Half of the world's reserves of this **precious metal** are in South Africa.

26

Malabo

EQUATORIAL GUINEA

SÃO TOMÉ AND PRÍNCIPE São Tomé

Libreville

GABON

CONGO

Brazzaville

Congo River

Cabinda Province (Angola) →

Kinshasa

The **National Bank of Angola** was built when Angola was still a colony of Portugal, but now the Angolan government owns it.

National Bank of Angola

Luanda

ANGOL

Swamp monkeys have pouches in their cheeks where they keep food.

swamp monkey

Guineafowl make their nests on the ground and eat ticks, spiders and lice.

guineafowl

San bushmen

ATLANTIC OCEAN

NAMIBI

Namib Desert

The sand dunes in the **Namib Desert** are some of the highest in the world.

Windhoek

rugby players

The Springboks, South Africa's national **rugby team**, hosted and won the World Cup in 1995. They won it again in 2007.

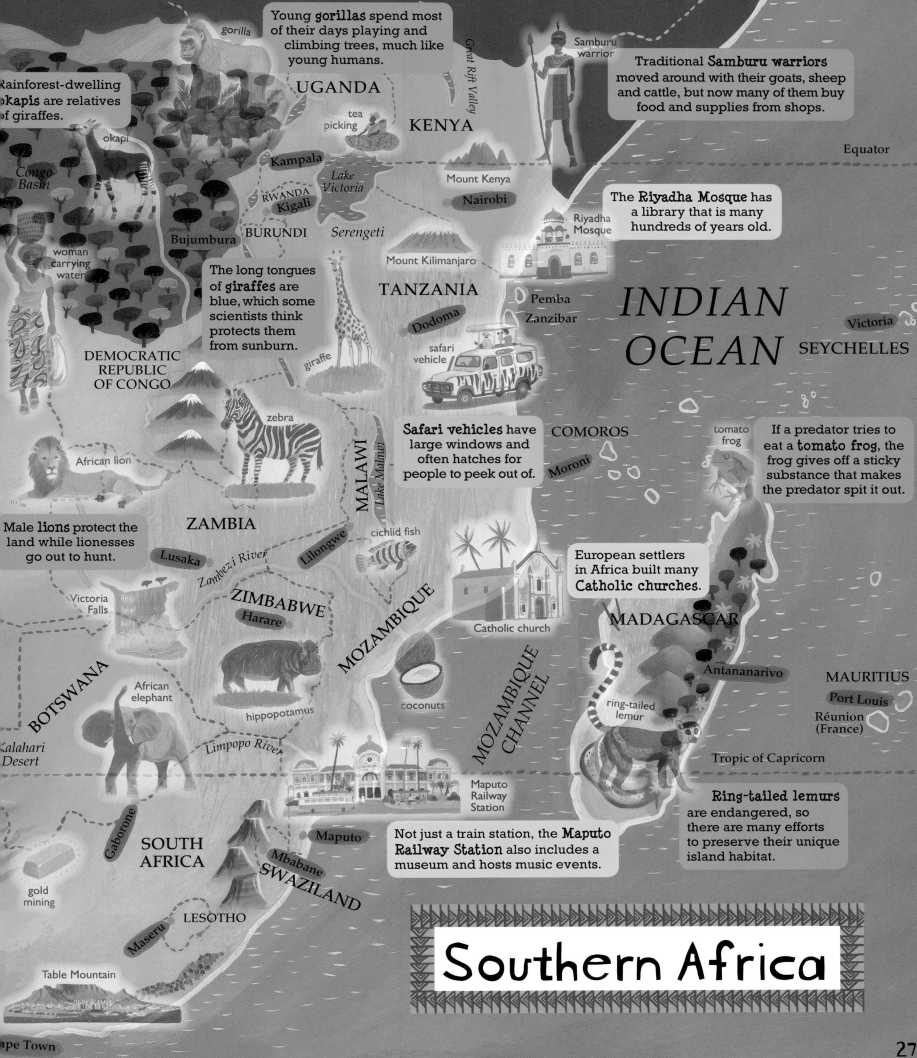

Young **gorillas** spend most of their days playing and climbing trees, much like young humans.

Rainforest-dwelling **okapis** are relatives of giraffes.

Traditional **Samburu warriors** moved around with their goats, sheep and cattle, but now many of them buy food and supplies from shops.

Samburu warrior

gorilla

UGANDA

Great Rift Valley

KENYA

Equator

tea picking

Kampala

Lake Victoria

Mount Kenya

okapi

Nairobi

RWANDA
Kigali

The **Riyadha Mosque** has a library that is many hundreds of years old.

Congo Basin

woman carrying water

BURUNDI
Bujumbura

Serengeti

Riyadha Mosque

The long tongues of **giraffes** are blue, which some scientists think protects them from sunburn.

Mount Kilimanjaro

DEMOCRATIC REPUBLIC OF CONGO

giraffe

TANZANIA

Pemba
Zanzibar

INDIAN OCEAN

Victoria

SEYCHELLES

Dodoma

safari vehicle

zebra

Safari vehicles have large windows and often hatches for people to peek out of.

COMOROS

tomato frog

If a predator tries to eat a **tomato frog**, the frog gives off a sticky substance that makes the predator spit it out.

African lion

Moroni

MALAWI
Lake Malawi

Male **lions** protect the land while lionesses go out to hunt.

ZAMBIA

cichlid fish

European settlers in Africa built many **Catholic churches**.

Lusaka

Zambezi River

Lilongwe

Victoria Falls

ZIMBABWE
Harare

MOZAMBIQUE

Catholic church

MADAGASCAR

BOTSWANA

African elephant

hippopotamus

coconuts

MOZAMBIQUE CHANNEL

Antananarivo

ring-tailed lemur

MAURITIUS

Port Louis

Réunion (France)

Kalahari Desert

Limpopo River

Tropic of Capricorn

Gaborone

SOUTH AFRICA

Maputo

Mbabane
SWAZILAND

Maputo Railway Station

Not just a train station, the **Maputo Railway Station** also includes a museum and hosts music events.

Ring-tailed lemurs are endangered, so there are many efforts to preserve their unique island habitat.

gold mining

LESOTHO
Maseru

Table Mountain

Southern Africa

Cape Town

People

This **girl's** Indigenous ancestors avoided the Spanish invaders by living deep in the Sierra Madre mountains.

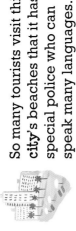

Which **sports player** shoots a hard rubber disc called a puck that travels at very fast speeds?

Plants & Animals

North Dakota produces half of America's supply of this **crop**, which usually becomes pasta.

Which **antlered animals** are the largest and heaviest members of the deer family?

European settlers hunted this **mammal** almost to extinction, but conservation efforts helped their population recover a little.

Which **insect**, unlike other types of butterflies, cannot survive cold winters, so must migrate south to stay warm?

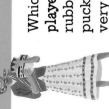

Landmarks

The Canadian National Railway funded the construction of this **tower** in Toronto, once the world's tallest free-standing structure.

What is the name of the **waterfalls** that formed at the end of the last ice age 12,000 years ago?

So many tourists visit this **city's** beaches that it has special police who can speak many languages.

Which **church** was built to look like an igloo? It is located in Inuvik, which is home to many Western Canadian Inuit people.

Activities & Transport

Using a steam-belt mechanism, these **facilities** scoop grain directly from ships and elevate it into huge storage bins.

Which monuments are carved from large trees by Indigenous peoples of the Pacific Northwest?

Can you find the elevated **vehicles** in Chicago that form America's fourth largest rapid transit system?

Indigenous peoples of the Arctic made these **sculptures of stones** for many different purposes.

North America

ARCTIC OCEAN

NORTH ASIA

BERING STRAIT

Alaska (USA)

Yukon River

Brooks Range

inukshuk

BEAUFORT SEA

Our Lady of Victory Church

Banks Island

Victoria Island

Queen Elizabeth Islands

purple saxifrage

Purple saxifrage plants only grow about two to four new leaves a year.

Arctic Circle

BAFFIN BAY

Inuit kayaker

The **Inuit people** invented kayaks, which can pass through water almost silently.

Baffin Island

DAVIS STRAIT

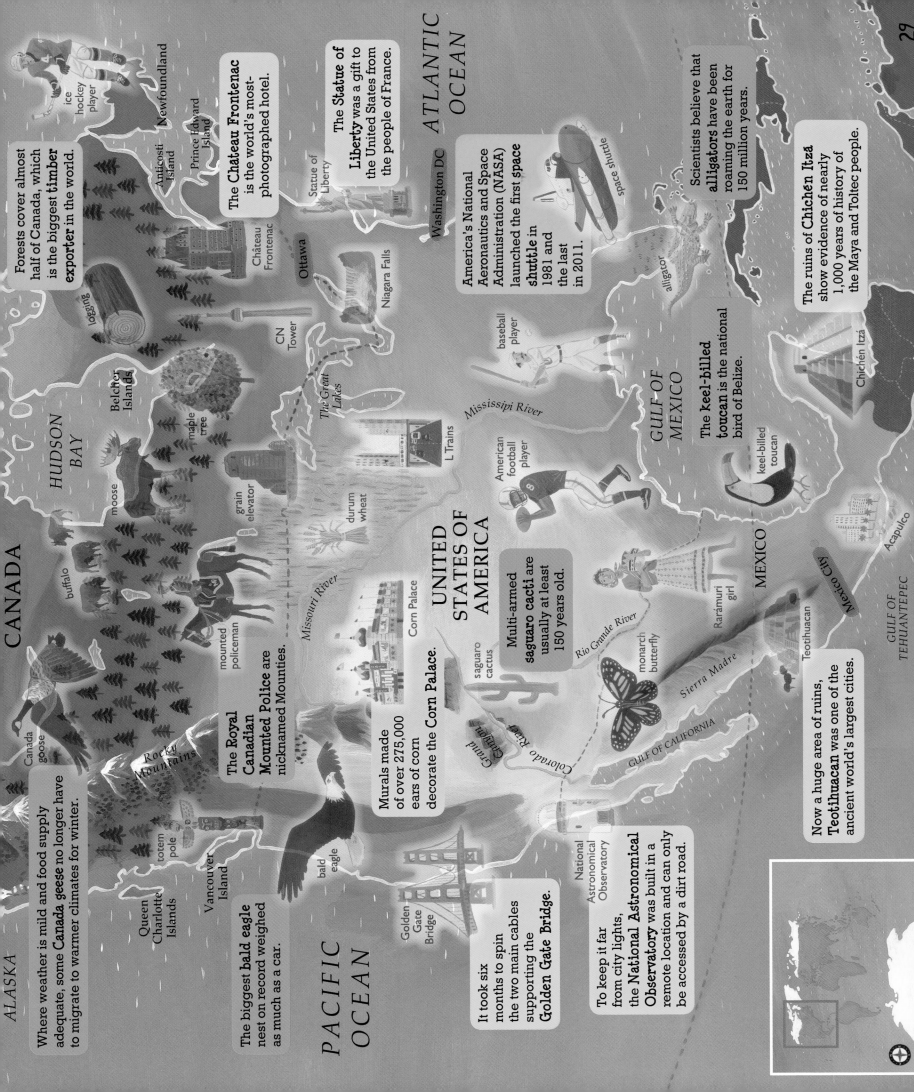

ALASKA

CANADA

PACIFIC OCEAN

UNITED STATES OF AMERICA

MEXICO

ATLANTIC OCEAN

GULF OF MEXICO

HUDSON BAY

GULF OF CALIFORNIA

GULF OF TEHUANTEPEC

Forests cover almost half of Canada, which is the biggest timber exporter in the world.

The Château Frontenac is the world's most-photographed hotel.

The Statue of Liberty was a gift to the United States from the people of France.

America's National Aeronautics and Space Administration (NASA) launched the first space shuttle in 1981 and the last in 2011.

Scientists believe that alligators have been roaming the earth for 150 million years.

The ruins of Chichén Itzá show evidence of nearly 1,000 years of history of the Maya and Toltec people.

The keel-billed toucan is the national bird of Belize.

Multi-armed saguaro cacti are usually at least 150 years old.

The Royal Canadian Mounted Police are nicknamed Mounties.

Murals made of over 275,000 ears of corn decorate the Corn Palace.

It took six months to spin the two main cables supporting the Golden Gate Bridge.

To keep it far from city lights, the National Astronomical Observatory was built in a remote location and can only be accessed by a dirt road.

The biggest bald eagle nest on record weighed as much as a car.

Where weather is mild and food supply adequate, some Canada geese no longer have to migrate to warmer climates for winter.

Now a huge area of ruins, **Teotihuacan** was one of the ancient world's largest cities.

ice hockey player

Newfoundland

Prince Edward Island

Anticosti Island

Statue of Liberty

Washington DC

Château Frontenac

Ottawa

CN Tower

Niagara Falls

space shuttle

alligator

Chichén Itzá

logging

Belcher Islands

maple tree

The Great Lakes

baseball player

keel-billed toucan

L Trains

Mississipi River

moose

buffalo

durum wheat

American football player

grain elevator

Corn Palace

saguaro cactus

Rio Grande River

monarch butterfly

Rarámuri girl

Mexico City

Acapulco

Teotihuacan

Sierra Madre

mounted policeman

Missouri River

totem pole

Rocky Mountains

Canada goose

Queen Charlotte Islands

Vancouver Island

Golden Gate Bridge

National Astronomical Observatory

bald eagle

Colorado River

Grand Canyon

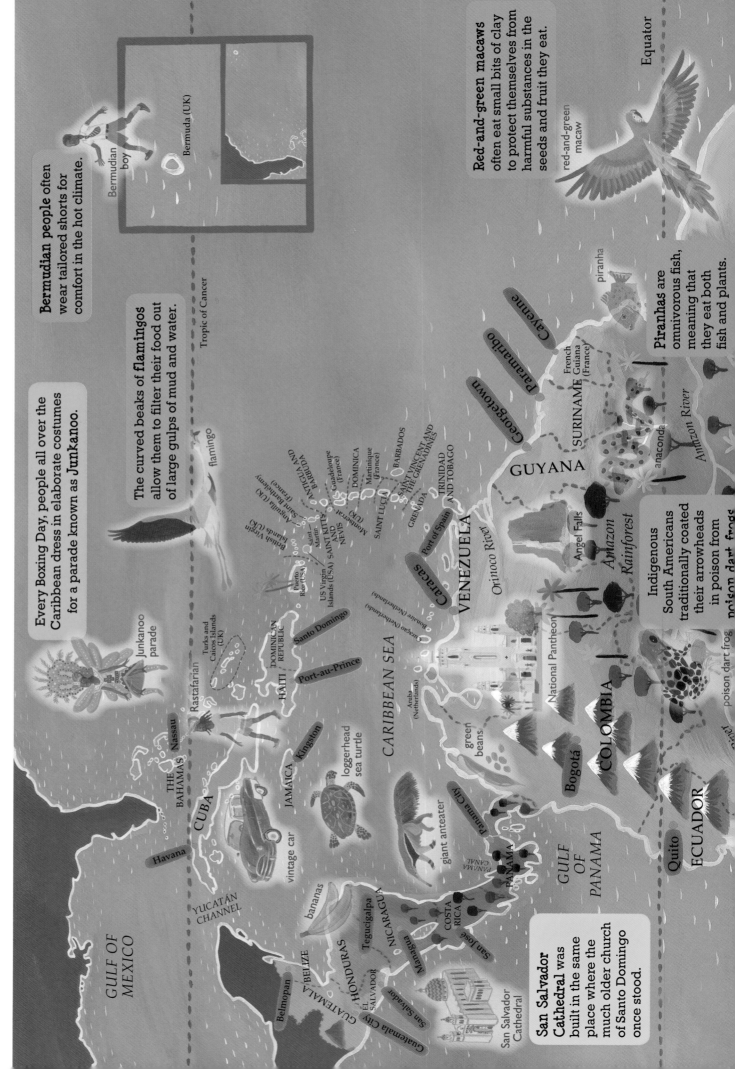

People

Which couple performs a **dance** known for its flowing movement and sudden stops and starts?

Plants & Animals

In the wild, these **reptiles** usually live for over 50 years, but they are still an endangered species.

Landmarks

This **waterfall** is the highest in the world — about 20 times higher than Niagara Falls.

Activities & Transport

 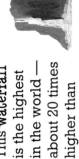

Paraguay has no coastline, but these **ships** patrol its large rivers.

Because the United States stopped trading with Cuba in 1960, most American **cars** there are very old.

Bermudian people often wear tailored shorts for comfort in the hot climate.

Bermudian boy

Bermuda (UK)

Red-and-green macaws often eat small bits of clay to protect themselves from harmful substances in the seeds and fruit they eat.

red-and-green macaw

Tropic of Cancer

Every Boxing Day, people all over the Caribbean dress in elaborate costumes for a parade known as **Junkanoo**.

The curved beaks of flamingos allow them to filter their food out of large gulps of mud and water.

flamingo

Piranhas are omnivorous fish, meaning that they eat both fish and plants.

piranha

Cayenne

Paramaribo

Georgetown

French Guiana (France)

SURINAME

GUYANA

anaconda

Amazon River

Equator

Junkanoo parade

Rastafarian

Turks and Caicos Islands (UK)

Puerto Rico (USA)

US Virgin Islands (USA)

British Virgin Islands (UK)

Saint Martin

Anguilla (UK)

Saint Barthélemy (France)

SAINT KITTS AND NEVIS

ANTIGUA AND BARBUDA

Montserrat (UK)

Guadeloupe (France)

DOMINICA

Martinique (France)

SAINT LUCIA

BARBADOS

SAINT VINCENT AND THE GRENADINES

GRENADA

TRINIDAD AND TOBAGO

Port of Spain

Curaçao (Netherlands)

Bonaire (Netherlands)

Aruba (Netherlands)

Caracas

VENEZUELA

Orinoco River

Angel Falls

Amazon Rainforest

National Pantheon

Indigenous South Americans traditionally coated their arrowheads in poison from poison dart frogs.

poison dart frog

green beans

COLOMBIA

Bogotá

THE BAHAMAS

Nassau

CUBA

Havana

JAMAICA

Kingston

loggerhead sea turtle

vintage car

HAITI

Port-au-Prince

DOMINICAN REPUBLIC

Santo Domingo

CARIBBEAN SEA

San Salvador Cathedral was built in the same place where the much older church of Santo Domingo once stood.

San Salvador Cathedral

GULF OF MEXICO

YUCATÁN CHANNEL

BELIZE

Belmopan

GUATEMALA

Guatemala City

HONDURAS

Tegucigalpa

EL SALVADOR

San Salvador

NICARAGUA

Managua

COSTA RICA

San José

bananas

PANAMA

Panama City

PANAMA CANAL

giant anteater

GULF OF PANAMA

ECUADOR

Quito

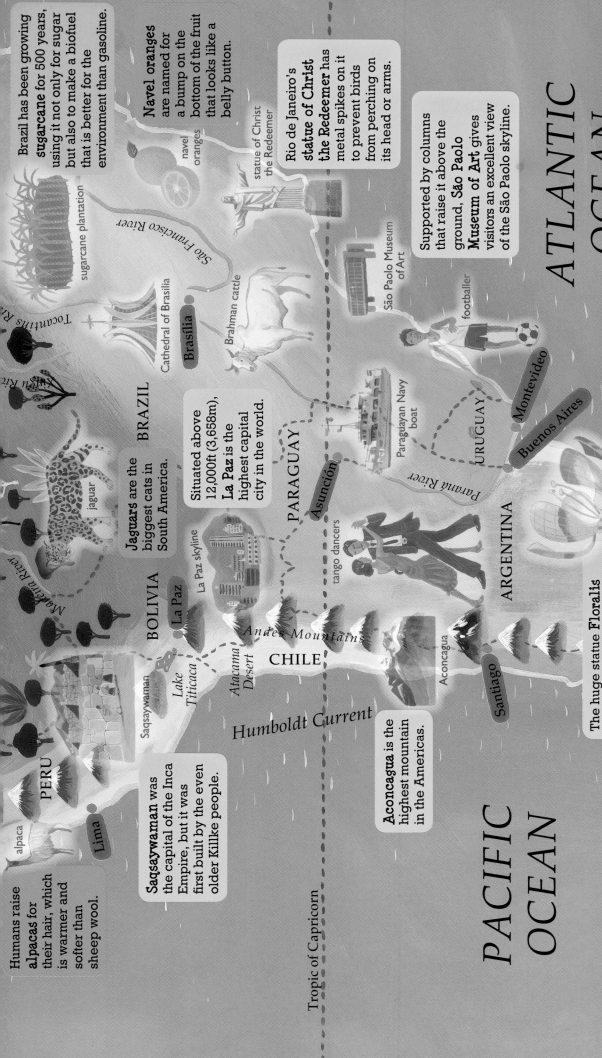

South America, Central America and the Caribbean

Brazil has been growing **sugarcane** for 500 years, using it not only for sugar but also to make a biofuel that is better for the environment than gasoline.

sugarcane plantation

Navel oranges are named for a bump on the bottom of the fruit that looks like a belly button.

navel oranges

statue of Christ the Redeemer

Rio de Janeiro's **statue of Christ the Redeemer** has metal spikes on it to prevent birds from perching on its head or arms.

Supported by columns that raise it above the ground, **São Paolo Museum of Art** gives visitors an excellent view of the São Paolo skyline.

São Paolo Museum of Art

footballer

ATLANTIC OCEAN

São Francisco River

Tocantins River

Cathedral of Brasília

Brasília

Brahman cattle

BRAZIL

Xingu River

Jaguars are the biggest cats in South America.

jaguar

Madeira River

Paraguayan Navy boat

Paraná River

Montevideo

Buenos Aires

URUGUAY

PARAGUAY

Asunción

Situated above 12,000ft (3,658m), **La Paz** is the highest capital city in the world.

tango dancers

La Paz skyline

BOLIVIA

La Paz

Saqsaywaman

Lake Titicaca

Andes Mountains

CHILE

Atacama Desert

Floralis Genérica

ARGENTINA

Humboldt Current

PERU

Lima

alpaca

Humans raise **alpacas** for their hair, which is warmer and softer than sheep wool.

Saqsaywaman was the capital of the Inca Empire, but it was first built by the even older Killke people.

Aconcagua

Aconcagua is the highest mountain in the Americas.

Santiago

The huge statue **Floralis Genérica** in Buenos Aires was designed to move, opening its petals every morning and closing them at night.

Gauchos, who are similar to cowboys, were known for capturing escaped livestock (like cattle) after Spanish settlers came to South America.

gaucho

Tierra del Fuego

Cape Horn

Falkland Islands (UK)

Tropic of Capricorn

PACIFIC OCEAN

There's more to explore!

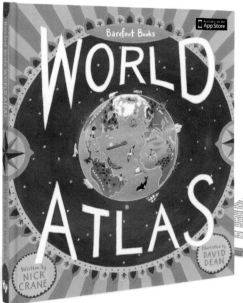

Delve deeper into the places you've visited in this sticker book in the award-winning *Barefoot Books World Atlas*. Find *World Atlas*, the Barefoot World Atlas app and additional global stories at *www.barefootbooks.com*.

Barefoot Books
2067 Massachusetts Ave
Cambridge, MA 02140

Barefoot Books
29/30 Fitzroy Square
London, W1T 6LQ

Graphic design by Sarah Soldano, Barefoot Books
Edited by Nivair H. Gabriel, Barefoot Books
and Emma Parkin, Conker House
Cartography by Stephen Raw, Manchester, UK
Reproduction by Bright Arts, Hong Kong
Printed in Malaysia
This book was typeset in Blockhead,
Minya Nouvelle, Palatino and Rockwell
The illustrations were prepared in acrylics

ISBN 978-1-78285-830-0

1 3 5 7 9 8 6 4 2

Editor's Note: As there are many different ways to spell and name the places of the world, for consistency we conformed to the spellings in *The Times Comprehensive Atlas of the World*.

ANTARCTICA

SOUTHERN OCEAN

submarine

cruise ship

seaplane

NORTH AMERICA

fishing boat

ASIA

PACIFIC OCEAN

ATLANTIC OCEAN

INDIAN OCEAN

outrigger canoe

oil tanker

OCEANIA

EUROPE

SOUTH AMERICA

passenger plane

bus

paddle steamer

AFRICA

ARCTIC OCEAN

freighter

container ship

PAGES 2–3

World Map

truck

bathyscaphe Trieste

beaked whale

albatross

sea otters

yelloweye rockfish

pearl oyster

dugong

Trinidad

swordfish

Great Pacific Garbage Patch

killer whale

volcanoes

bluefin tuna

Great Barrier Reef

Taranaki Basin

iceberg

sea lion

bowhead whale

person paddling canoe

leatherback turtle

Atlantic and Arctic Oceans

Arctic drift station

Nenets people

Yup'ik mask

beluga whale

Vikings

Fram

aurora borealis

tundra swan

haddock

snow goose

Arctic fox

Gjøa

walrus

Arctic tern

narwhal

North Pole

peregrine falcon

grey wolf

blue whale

musk ox

Titanic

swallow

Atlantic cod

Magellanic penguin

icebreaker

bottlenose dolphin

Felicity Ann

marine iguana

Pacific Ocean

school of common dolphins

pirogue

Inuit girl

Double Eagle V

Kon-Tiki

salmon

puffin

Trans-Alaska pipeline

giant squid

Easter Island statues

Uummannaq

polar bear

icebreaker

lantern fish

mackerel

fur seal

Patagonian toothfish

underwater government meeting

Vostok Station

angelfish

whale shark

king crab

RRS *Discovery*

Antarctic petrel

Adélie penguins

scuba diver

South Pole

mackerel icefish

hawksbill turtle

dogsled team

polar transport vehicle

tsunami

southern bluefin tuna

krill

Southern right whale

converted tractors

sardines

emperor penguin

oil rig

leopard seals

PAGES 8–9

Indian Ocean, Southern Ocean and Antarctica

Mauna Kea Observatories

Uluru (Ayers Rock)

wine making

platypus

Tahitian dancer

great white shark

flying doctors

tuna

kiwi

rugby players

opal mining

red-knobbed hornbill

Angkor Wat

Sultan's Palace

coffee plantation

Vietnamese cyclist

statue of the Buddha

palm oil plantation

orangutan

Buddhist monk

Schwedagon Pagoda

Petronas Towers

orchid

Borobodur

tuk-tuk

Sumatran elephant

Malayan tapir

komodo dragon

Turtle Tower

butterflies

tree kangaroo

dwarf cuscus

Balinese dancer

Wat Phra Kaew

Sumatran tiger

Banaue rice terraces

Great Dividing Range

Perth skyline

HMS Bounty

jeepney bus

sulphur-crested cockatoo

Southern Alps

slit drum

great frigatebird

sheep farmer

green sea turtle

kangaroo

horned parakeet

surfer

king bird of paradise

gold mining

Sydney Opera House

manta ray

bamboo

Hwaseong Fortress

Kinkaku-ji

Changchun car manufacturing

yak

Hong Kong skyline

Forbidden City

Chinese junk

Japanese crane

jade

novice Buddhist monks

tae kwon do

bullet train

pineapple

Oriental Pearl Tower, Shanghai

torii gate

Tokyo skyscapers

Great Wall of China

children playing table tennis

golden snub-nosed monkey

rice paddies

Three Gorges Dam

panda

coal mining

PAGES 14–15
East Asia

Potala Palace

Changdeokgung

Donghai Bridge Wind Farm

oil fields in the Qaidam Basin

Russian man and girl

brown bear

European mink

wheat

Trans-Siberian Railway

coal mining

ballerina

reindeer

Turkmen boy

volcanoes of Kamchatka

yurt

Sher-Dor Madrasah

Siberian tiger

Soyuz rocket

Ambassador car

sacred cow

blue houses of Jodhpur

tea pickers

snow leopard

boy playing cricket

Bombay stock exchange

bathers in the Ganges

Indian elephant

Mausoleum of Quaid-e-Azam

Sri Lankan stilt fisherman

South Asia
PAGES 18–19

Mausoleum of Timur Shah

Sri Lankan girl

Bengal tiger

Indian peacock

Friday Mosque

Taj Mahal

Gateway of India

woman carrying water

sacred fig tree

Kapaleeshwarar Temple

Boudhanath Stupa

North and Central Asia
PAGES 16–17

Golden Temple

banyan tree

water buffalo and egret

Dalmatian pelican

walrus

snow crane

pumpjack

Bactrian camel

Urengoy gas field

petroglyphs

combine harvester

Saint Basil's Cathedral

Winter Palace, Saint Petersburg

Genghis Khan

snowy owl

Lady Maslenitsa

Blue Mosque

figs

fishing boat

northern bald ibis

Cypriot Navy patrol boat

apricots

frankincense tree

Omani man

Shah Mosque

Burj Al Arab Hotel

Iranian girl

date palms

striped hyena

Jvari Monastery

oil fields

Great Mosque of Samarra

Southwest Asia
PAGES 20–21

Palmyra

kestrel

Library of Celsus

Mecca

Yerevan Cascade

pomegranate farm

Eurasian lynx

Old Walled City of Shibam

Petra

Imam Ali Mosque, Najif

Arabian horse

Jebel Barkal

lady going to market

baboon

Berber goatherd

tea

cocoa beans

Great Pyramid

black crowned crane

African wild dog

martial eagle

African spurred tortoise

Great Mosque of Djenné

Imohag

scorpion

giant African snail

Europe
PAGES 22–23

Big Ben
skier
Cossack dancer
pysanka (decorated egg)
cow
fallow deer
grapes
Mt. Etna
Sami woman
Scottish boy
Colosseum
timber-frame house
Saint Sophia Cathedral
olive tree
the Alps
geyser
La Giralda
Parthenon
Stonehenge
raspberry
children playing football
wind turbine
lavender fields
miner
wild boar
Leaning Tower of Pisa
Eiffel Tower
Brandenburg Gate
Rubik's Cube
Sagrada Família
Bran Castle

Chad-Cameroon oil pipeline
lighthouse
gazelle
cobra
Sudanese children
Church of Saint George
Nile crocodile
Hassan Tower
Burj Al-Fateh Hotel
ancient Egyptians
locust
Guinean boy
felucca boat
chimpanzee
Emi Koussi
tbal player
Lion of Judah monument
Tunisian boy
Cairo skyline
one-humped dromedary camel
baobab tree
Leptis Magna

North Africa
PAGES 24–25

Victoria Falls

Namib Desert

okapi

tea picking

rugby players

swamp monkey

Samburu warrior

Mount Kenya

tomato frog

gold mining

gorilla

woman carrying water

coconuts

African elephant

cichlid fish

Catholic church

zebra

giraffe

National Bank of Angola

Maputo Railway Station

ring-tailed lemur

safari vehicle

Southern Africa PAGES 26–27

San bushmen

guineafowl

hippopotamus

Mount Kilimanjaro

Riyadha Mosque

Table Mountain

African lion

Paraguayan Navy boat

Angel Falls

anaconda

piranha

La Paz skyline

Cathedral of Brasilia

Bermudian boy

green beans

National Pantheon

alpaca

navel oranges

Junkanoo parade

Saqsaywaman

Brahman cattle

tango dancers

statue of Christ the Redeemer

sugarcane plantation

Corn Palace

buffalo

Teotihuacan

totem pole

durum wheat

Rarámuri girl

Château Frontenac

American football player

mounted policeman

bald eagle

logging

grain elevator

Our Lady of Victory Church

saguaro cactus

ice hockey player

space shuttle

Statue of Liberty

baseball player

Inuit kayaker

CN Tower

Chichén Itzá

moose

L Trains

North America

PAGES 28–29

keel-billed toucan

Niagara Falls

inukshuk

Acapulco

maple tree

monarch butterfly

alligator

purple saxifrage

Golden Gate Bridge

Canada goose

footballer

giant anteater

National Astronomical Observatory

Rastafarian

bananas

flamingo

loggerhead sea turtle

São Paolo Museum of Art

San Salvador Cathedral

gaucho

PAGES 30–31

vintage car

red-and-green macaw

Floralis Genérica

poison dart frog

South America, Central America and the Caribbean